Geochemistry and Petrology of the Rocky Hill Stock, Tulare County, California

George W. Putman
State University of New York at Albany, Albany, New York

and

John T. Alfors
California Division of Mines and Geology,
San Francisco, California

THE
GEOLOGICAL SOCIETY
OF AMERICA

SPECIAL PAPER 120

Published by
THE GEOLOGICAL SOCIETY OF AMERICA, INC.
Colorado Building, P. O. Box 1719
Boulder, Colorado 80302

Printed in the United States of America

*The printing of this volume has been made possible
through the bequest of
Richard Alexander Fullerton Penrose, Jr.,
and is partially supported by a grant from
The National Science Foundation.*

Acknowledgments

We wish to express our appreciation to Prof. O. F. Tuttle, Stanford University, for reviews of earlier versions of the manuscript; to Prof. B. W. Evans, University of California, Berkeley, for electron probe microanalyses of biotite; to Acton Laboratories, Inc., for electron probe microanalyses of plagioclase and magnetite; to Prof. F. J. Turner, University of California, Berkeley, for some of the universal stage determinations of plagioclase compositions; and to Dr. Hans Seck, Stanford University, for making X-ray diffractometer measurements of potassium feldspar. Dr. H. W. Oliver, U. S. Geological Survey, kindly provided regional gravity data. Use of a magnetic susceptibility bridge was provided by Utah Construction and Mining Company. Computer time for the trend-surface analyses was donated by Western Data Processing, Inc.; programs were made available through the courtesy of Prof. D. B. McIntyre, Pomona College; and the data were processed with the assistance of D. D. Pollard, Stanford University. Facilities for hydrothermal experiments were provided through the courtesy of Prof. O. F. Tuttle and Dean R. H. Jahns, Stanford University, and runs were carried out with the guidance of J. H. Carman.

We gratefully acknowledge the assistance of our colleagues, Dr. R. H. Chapman for the gravity and magnetometer studies, Dr. Matti Tavela for the ferrous-ferric iron analyses, Dr. E. B. Gross for X-ray diffraction studies, Mrs. L. A. Lofgren and C. B. Smith for assistance in sample preparation and data compilation, and L. A. Readdy for assistance in sample collection.

Helpful critical reviews of the manuscript were provided by Profs. Robert H. Osborne and Gregory A. Davis, University of Southern California. Finally, we wish to express our appreciation to the property owners in the area for granting access to their land.

Contents

FIGURES

PLATES

TABLES

Abstract

The Rocky Hill granodiorite stock is a relatively homogeneous, epizonal pluton which is texturally zoned into a medium-grained, granitic-textured rim-facies and a fine- to medium-grained, subporphyritic core-facies. It is about 1.5 square miles in area and intrudes metamorphosed ultramafic and metavolcanic rocks on the western edge of the Sierra Nevada 12.5 miles southeast of Visalia, California. The exposed contacts of the stock are sharp and steeply dipping. Apophyses and dikes into the wall rocks are present, but few. Although outcrops of the granodiorite appear to be massive, a weak, steeply plunging lineation is generally present. In addition, a northwest-trending planar grain fracture, which is most easily observed on weathered surfaces, parallels the most prominent set of joints. Aplite dikes of various sizes, up to a maximum of 10 feet thick and 4000 feet long, occur throughout the stock; small irregular aplitic segregations are common in rocks of the core-facies. Sparse ellipsoidal inclusions up to 3 feet long are present in most outcrops of the rim-facies granodiorite but are exceedingly rare in the core-facies granodiorite. The effects of protoclastic deformation are found throughout the stock but are most intensive in the rim-facies granodiorite. Limited deuteric alteration has affected rocks of both facies, but the zone of most intense chloritization as well as areas with higher sulfide contents are within or close to the core-facies.

Rock samples from 151 localities were collected on an equal-interval (375 feet), orthogonal grid over the entire stock and were used with additional samples to determine the within-pluton (regional) and within-grid variation in trace-element content of the ferromagnesian minerals as well as the variation in petrographic properties. Modal analyses show that rim-facies rocks are characterized by higher hornblende, slightly higher potassium feldspar, and slightly lower plagioclase and quartz contents than the core-facies rocks. Within-hand-specimen variation constitutes a large portion of the total modal variation, especially in the rim-facies rocks, and distribution patterns of the modal minerals could not be effectively determined (except for magnetite) by the sampling design used in this study. Chemical analyses of composite samples of rim- and core-facies granodiorite are similar, but the small differences are consistent with modal differences between rock-facies. Spectro-chemical analyses of ferromagnesian mineral separates contain significant regional variation trends, specifically a progressive decrease inward from the walls of the stock in the contents of Be, Cr, V, and Ni, and an erratic increase in Cu and Zn. In preparing regional patterns for Cr, Cu, Ni, V, and Zn, it was necessary to correct the ferromagnesian data for the influence of the modal distribution of co-existing magnetite.

Field and laboratory evidence indicate that the Rocky Hill stock was emplaced as a single, nearly vertical intrusion of relatively fluid granodiorite magma (less than 20 percent crystals) which crystallized progressively inward from the walls. When approximately 75 percent of the stock (at the present level of exposure) consisted of solid or nearly solid granodiorite (rim-facies rocks), saturation in volatiles occurred, and isothermal pressure quenching ensued to produce the matrix of the core-facies granodiorite. Portions of the solid rim and newly crystallized core ruptured, and some of the still-fluid, residual magma in the core area was intruded into the fractures as aplite dikes. Temperature of the magma at the time of initial intrusion, as estimated from biotite composition and petrographic evidence, was probably near 850°C; at the time of final consolidation it was probably less than 700°C. Petrographic and field evidence suggests that, at the time of aplite intrusion, water pressure equaled load pressure. A comparison of the composition of the aplites with the position of the quaternary isobaric liquidus minimum in the system $NaAlSi_3O_8$-$KAlSi_3O_8$-SiO_2-H_2O indicates that a water pressure of 1.5 to 2 kb existed when the aplites were emplaced. An estimated depth of intrusion of the Rocky Hill stock is 5.5 to 7 km.

A model for the intrusion which is a vertical cylinder 7,000 feet in diameter with a depth exceeding 16,000 feet is consistent with a gravity anomaly over the stock.

Introduction

GENERAL STATEMENT—REGIONAL VARIATION IN GRANITIC ROCKS

In recent years an increasing amount of attention has been turned to the quantitative description of various properties of granitic rocks on an areal or regional basis. Such information is potentially useful in answering questions about the petrology and petrogenesis of granitic rocks, as well as in solving problems concerning the relative movement of crustal units involving batholithic masses (Whitten, 1961; Baird and others, 1966). A critical aspect of this work lies in defining the relationship between scale in a rock unit and the variation of a particular property of the rock unit as measured in samples from it. This situation has been aptly stated by Whitten (1961) and discussed by Baird and others (1964). The latter authors have been specifically concerned with major chemical constituents of igneous rocks, but their conclusions have general relevance for the regional description of any rock property and bear repeating here.

> Some rock types increase in variability directly and markedly with scale and others show such high variability at the small scale that it is difficult to detect any increase by sampling over larger areas. The implication of these facts for evaluation of compositional trends is clear: without estimates of smaller scale variability it is not possible to judge the significance of large scale variations (Baird and others, 1964, p. 259).

Unfortunately, information on variability versus scale was, until recently, virtually nonexistent for most properties of geologic interest in granitic rock masses. Largely through the intensive efforts of Baird and others (1964, 1966, 1967a, 1967b) and Richmond (1965) in studying the variation of major chemical constituents of granitic rocks, and of Emerson (1964) and Welday and Baird (1966) in regard to modal mineral variations, the first quantitative estimates have been made of the behavior of these properties on different scales in specific plutonic units.

3

Our studies of metal distributions in granitic rocks have led us along roughly parallel paths in regard to a concern for regional distribution data, but with somewhat more emphasis upon other variable properties of the rock. Earlier reconnaissance sampling of granitic rock units in Arizona at approximately 1-mile intervals indicated that minor and trace element contents of ferromagnesian mineral phase(s) of each separate plutonic unit constituted an identifiable attribute of the rock unit—much as a compositional "fingerprint" (Putman and Burnham, 1963). However, in that study no information was obtained concerning the distribution of this compositional variability at any smaller scale within a rock unit, or upon the two-dimensional aspects of such variability at any scale.

OBJECTIVES OF THIS STUDY—SELECTION OF THE ROCKY HILL STOCK

A fuller understanding of compositional variation in granitic rocks logically requires that it be related to the petrogenesis or crystallization history of the body or bodies of concern. To explore this relationship, we undertook to study the compositional variability of a relatively simple granitic body with a sampling plan designed to extract regional[1] data on minor element distribution in ferromagnesian mineral phases. This particular emphasis resulted from a desire to optimize analytical precision, to reduce the effects of modal variation, and to obtain data on possible fractionation trends by using suitable metals, such as Cr, Ni, and V, which commonly occur in ferromagnesian phases. Concomitant with sampling and subsequent analytical work on rock and mineral samples, field and petrographic determinations were made of other rock properties, both at sample collection sites and at other localities.

A prime objective was to derive the emplacement and crystallization history of this rock body from the information gained from a number of rock properties. Hopefully, this petrogenetic picture would be consistent with, derive significant support from, and possibly gain additional detail from the regional minor element distribution data, thus providing an index of the value of this type of data. An account of the results of this project, which was carried out on the Rocky Hill stock in Tulare County, California, forms the basis for this paper.

Selection of the Site of this Study

A number of criteria were considered in the selection of a granitic body for this study, but the principal requirement was to select, insofar as possible,

---

[1]We use the term "regional" here in a more statistical than geologic sense. The "region" may be an area within one rock unit, as in this study.

a single homogeneous rock unit whose exposed surface best approximated a section completely through the unit. Accordingly, the following were considered the main factors in determining the final choice.

(1) The chosen pluton should be a petrologically simple granitic rock and not a composite body or product of multiple intrusion, nor a body exhibiting strong fractionation or segregation features.

(2) The body should possess a large proportion of outcrop.

(3) To limit the time required for field study, sampling, and analytical study, the body should be relatively small and accessible. Four square miles was considered the maximum area.

(4) Topographic relief should be low to minimize any effect on the regional data due to different levels of erosion.

(5) Hydrothermal or deuteric alteration should be slight so that primary compositional or other variation which results from the crystallization history is not unduly disturbed by later changes. The same criterion would also apply to possible postcrystallization metamorphism.

The Rocky Hill stock was selected as the plutonic body which most completely satisfied the above criteria, although its choice represented a certain degree of compromise from these criteria.

GEOLOGIC SETTING OF THE ROCKY HILL AREA

The Rocky Hill stock is a small, epizonal granodiorite pluton located about 12 miles southeast of Visalia, and 3 miles east of Exeter in Tulare County, California (Fig. 1), and in an area included within the U. S. Geological Survey's Rocky Hill, 7.5 minute quadrangle, (1951). The stock lies in the Sierra Nevada foothills 3 miles west of the main Sierra Nevada batholith. The stock forms a moderate hill from which it is named, with a maximum relief of 1000 ft, rising from a base level of approximately 600 ft. In plan, the stock is roughly circular with an area of about 1.5 square miles and is generally well exposed.

The stock is emplaced in a regionally metamorphosed rock series which includes metavolcanic rocks, metamorphosed basic igneous rocks (metagabbro), metasedimentary rocks, and serpentinized ultramafic rocks. Thermal or contact metamorphism is superimposed on these rocks adjacent to the Sierra Nevada batholith. The extent of contact metamorphism is difficult to recognize in metavolcanic rocks in the field. In the metasedimentary and serpentinized ultramafic rocks, contact metamorphic effects are generally restricted to within 1000 ft of the contacts of the Sierra Nevada batholith. Contact metamorphism related to the batholith does not appear to have affected any of the metamorphic rocks in the vicinity of the Rocky Hill stock .

feet. Portions of several grid lines were surveyed with compass and tape, and additional grid localities were located by resection.

Estimates of smaller scale or local variability in this work were derived from comparisons of duplicate samples collected at 25 grid localities, triplicate samples at one locality, four samples from grid square centers along line 2N, and seven samples collected at sequential intervals from one outcrop. A pooled estimate (Youden, 1951) of local variability was prepared from all these replicate samples since the distance between replicate samples did not seem to be significant; that is, duplicate samples collected 3 feet apart may show differences as large (or as small) as those collected 150 feet apart. This pooled estimate of local variability contains all contributions to variability arising at the within-grid square and smaller scales down to that of the individual sample, and can be thought of as variation occurring within a large outcrop. This estimate of local variability of a given property is hereafter referred to as *within-grid* variance in contrast to the *within-pluton* or total variance which is derived from data at all grid locations. This sampling plan was also used to obtain frequency distribution information for some minor elements within a mineral phase (Putman and Alfors, 1967).

Within the confines of practicality, every effort was made to obtain unbiased samples. Samples weighing 3 to 4 kg were taken from surface outcrops as close to the grid intersections as condition of the rock and physical limitations permitted. Initial sampling was made by means of a sledge and bull set. Visual inspection was made of the rock fragments, and, if the material appeared to be more than incipiently weathered, the outcrops were drilled and blasted. Drill holes were provided by a portable pneumatic hammer equipped with 1-inch diameter carbide bits. Most samples were collected within 30 to 100 feet of the grid point, and, in the case of dynamited outcrops, within 6 feet of the outcrop surface. In general, where duplicate samples were taken, one was collected by sledge and the other by blasting. All seven of the samples from a single outcrop (north of 2N-7W) were obtained by blasting. Samples were collected free of inclusions, aplites, and veins, and they were trimmed to remove obviously weathered material. Additional samples not indicated in Figure 2 were taken from inclusions, aplite dikes, minor altered phases of the granodiorite, and from serpentine, metagabbro, and amphibolite wall rocks.

Textural and modal observations in the field were supplemented by examination of stained rock slabs and standard thin sections of each rock sample. Variations in the chemical composition of bulk rocks and mineral phase separates were determined by emission and X-ray fluorescence spectroscopy, with particular emphasis upon analyses of selected trace elements in ferromagnesian phase separates from all grid samples on the stock. Compositional variation within individual mineral grains and identification of some inclusions was made or confirmed by electron microprobe analysis. Data on the relative oxidation state of iron in selected rock and mineral samples were derived from "wet" chemical ferrous-ferric iron determinations. Physical measurements included gravity and magnetometer surveys on the stock and adjacent area, and specific gravity and magnetic susceptibility determinations of bulk rock samples; the latter measurements were used to determine modal magnetite.

Geology and Internal Structure
of the Stock

GEOLOGY

A generalized geologic map of the stock is shown in Figure 2. About half of the contact of the stock is concealed by soil, colluvium, and slope wash material. Magnetometer traverses were helpful in locating some portions of the buried contact, but in other areas results were ambiguous because of the variable magnetite content of the granodiorite relative to the surrounding ultramafic rocks. However, by analogy to the dispersion of boulders and granitic detritus in areas where the contact is exposed, and by the gross symmetry of fractionation patterns (to be discussed subsequently), it is felt that the concealed contacts are within a few hundred feet of the nearest outcrop of the rock.

The exposed contacts of the stock are sharp and steeply dipping, but rather irregular in detailed map plan. Apophyses of granodiorite along the contacts are relatively few, but were noted near grid localities 0-9W, 4S-9W, southeast of 10S-3E (all in ultramafic rocks), 8N-9W (in metagabbro), and north of the stock along Rocky Hill Road between 1W and 3W (in metavolcanic rocks). The apophysis near 10S-3E is the largest observed, has a maximum width of approximately 10 feet, and exceeds 400 feet in length.

Two facies of granodiorite have been recognized for map and petrologic purposes. These are respectively referred to as the rim- and core-facies granodiorite on the basis of their spatial arrangement within the pluton. The bulk of the stock (rim-facies) is a medium-grained, inequigranular but granitic-textured granodiorite (Pl. 1, fig. 1). The granodiorite of the core-facies is finer-grained and is characterized by a subporphyritic texture (Pl. 1, fig. 2). The contact between these facies is transitional, over 100 feet or more, and some of the rocks mapped as core-facies granodiorite in Figure 2 exhibit transitional characteristics.

11

Figure 1. Photomicrograph of rim-facies granodiorite (sample 1N-8W), Rocky Hill stock, showing large perthitic potassium feldspar grains, subhedral plagioclase, and quartz. X6. Crossed nicols.

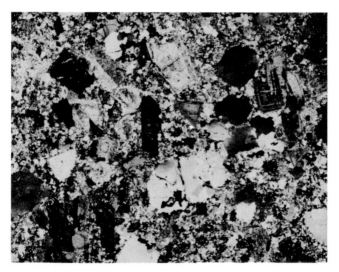

Figure 2. Photomicrograph of core-facies granodiorite (sample 2N-1E), Rocky Hill stock, showing phenocrysts of plagioclase and quartz set in a fine-grained matrix of potassium feldspar, quartz and albite. X6. Crossed nicols.

PHOTOMICROGRAPH OF RIM- AND CORE-FACIES
GRANODIORITE

PUTMAN AND ALFORS, PLATE 1
The Geological Society of America Special Paper 119

Aplite dikes of various sizes are common within the stock, and a generalized plot of the major dikes is shown in Figure 2. In addition, small aplitic segregations a few inches to several feet long and of nebulous form, some with small inner pegmatites, are common in many outcrops of corefacies rocks. Most aplite dikes have steep dips (70° to 90°) and sharply defined walls, although septa or screens of granodiorite parallel to the walls occur in the thicker dikes. Usually the thicker dikes are finer-grained adjacent to the walls; they frequently exhibit flow banding parallel to the walls as shown by alignment of mineral grains; and, with the exception of the dike series in the northwest portion of the stock, they become thinner when followed outward from the core area of the stock. None of the aplite dikes were observed to persist outward past the margins of the stock; but as exposures are poor locally, this cannot be ruled out. Small, simple pegmatite bodies are occasionally found within some dikes—most abundantly in those extending toward the northwest margin. Other features of the aplite dikes have been described previously (Putman and Alfors, 1965).

Inclusions are present in most outcrops of the rim-facies granodiorite, but they are not abundant. They are commonly oval or discoid in shape, usually with sharp boundaries, and range in size from a few inches to 6 feet in the maximum dimension. Elongate inclusions tend to be oriented parallel to a lineation in the surrounding granodiorite. With the exception of an 8-inch long inclusion of amphibolite, and one 6-foot long inclusion of mica schist near the southeast margin of the stock (vicinity 7S-5E), country rocks of the pluton were not recognized as inclusions. Measurements on a number of rim-facies outcrops indicate an average inclusion density of about 30 per 1000 square m. Inclusions are very rare in core-facies rocks, with an observed density of less than 1.5 per 1000 square m.

Other rock units in the stock include small quartz veins (maximum length 175 ft, vicinity 1S-1E) and pods (vicinity 2N-4E, 10S-1W), and a series of peculiar en echelon, steeply dipping, resistant dike-like bodies near grid locality 3S-6W. These "pseudo-dikes," as we will refer to them in subsequent discussion, are short linear or rib-like bodies whose maximum length is less than 150 feet for each member of the series, with a maximum thickness of about 10 feet. The pseudo-dikes have completely gradational boundaries with adjacent rim-facies granodiorite and median quartz veins generally less than 1 inch thick.

Although outcrops cover much of the assumed map area of the stock, many are weathered to varying degrees and pose problems in obtaining fresh samples close to a grid locality. Rock exposed in a riprap quarry at 7N-8W reveals irregular weathering which penetrates inward from a few inches to more than 8 feet from the surface of the outcrop. Many outcrops on less steep portions of the stock, unless disturbed by spalling or "plucking" of boulders bounded by joint planes, are likely to be weathered to even greater depths. In all, 42 of the 151 grid localities were sampled by drilling and blasting in an attempt to obtain fresher material. Some seemingly unweathered outcrops, which were blasted several days after rains, proved to be uniformly "wet" along grain boundaries or grain fracture surfaces for the entire exposed depth of up to 8 feet.

In spite of these sampling problems, comparisons of somewhat weathered samples and blasted samples from the same grid locality provided adequate control on possible bias in analyses due to weathering, and also indicated that bias arising from the choice of sample site at the grid locality (that is, if sources of fresher rock were compositionally or physically different from outcrops which are now more weathered) was highly unlikely.

INTERNAL STRUCTURE OF THE STOCK

Megascopic structural features which can be observed in outcrops on the stock include lineation, rare foliation, protoclastic shear, joints, planar grain fracturing, and late-stage fracturing. Lineation, foliation, protoclastic shear, and late fracturing can be classed as primary structural elements which developed during the intrusion of the stock and accompanying crystallization, whereas planar grain fracturing and joints are later structural elements apparently formed in entirely solid rock. These latter elements probably developed in large part at the time of emplacement of the younger Sierra Nevada batholith to the east.

Outcrops of the granodiorite are typically massive, and the spacing of joint planes and less common sheeting fractures tends to produce large blocks which become rounded by weathering and spalling along the edges. Attitudes of major joint sets and mineral lineations are plotted in Figure 3. The most prominent joint set of the stock strikes northwest and dips steeply northeast. It coincides with a major planar grain fracture which pervades most rocks in the stock. Locally, other joint orientations are predominant and control the appearance of outcrops. The northwest-striking joint set at Rocky Hill appears to be but one element in a northwest regional orientation of diverse structures of different ages in the foothill metamorphic belt. Beyond Rocky Hill these structures include joints, granitic and aplitic dikes near but outside the contact of the younger dominantly tonalitic batholith, still younger shear cleavage in some of these dikes, and the common strike direction of foliation in metavolcanic rocks and mica schists of the adjacent area (Fig. 1; Alfors and Putman, 1966).

Planar grain fracture is most easily observed on weathered outcrop surfaces, where it appears as a pronounced alignment of small fracture surfaces

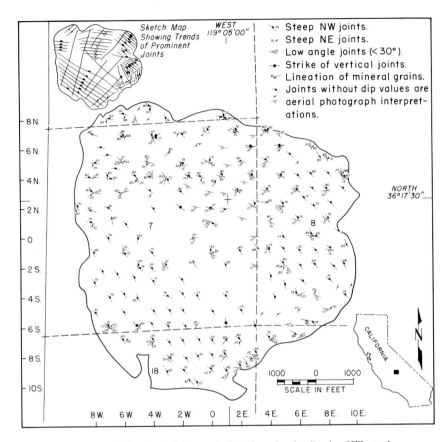

Figure 3. Attitude of joints and lineations in the Rocky Hill stock.

in quartz and feldspar grains. Individual fractures are confined to, at most, a few adjacent grains, but the over-all trend of many separate fractures constitutes a planar element which can readily be measured (Pl. 2, fig. 1).

A steeply plunging lineation is present in most outcrops and is defined by a crude preferred orientation of hornblende grains and ferromagnesian grain aggregates. On stained rock slabs a similar tendency for coincident crude alignment of elongated plagioclase grains, quartz aggregates, and elongate patches of anhedral potassium feldspar can be observed. Near-vertical lineation defined by biotite grains and quartz phenocrysts is also present in several of the thicker aplite dikes.

The effects of protoclastic deformation are found in varying degrees everywhere in the stock. The main effects are most easily observed in thin

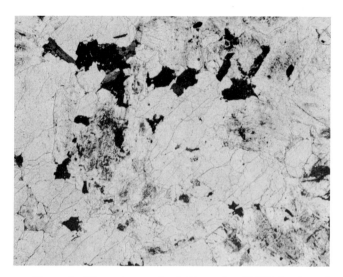

Figure 1. Photomicrograph of thin section 5S-8W showing sub-parallel late fractures, especially in the quartz grains. X6. Plane polarized light.

Figure 2. Photomicrograph of thin section 6S-7E showing embayed core of plagioclase, broken and displaced fragments of plagioclase veined by quartz, potassium feldspar, and minor biotite. Composition of plagioclase core is $An_{40\pm3}$ and that of the outermost zone of the margin is $An_{8\pm3}$. X20. Crossed nicols.

PHOTOMICROGRAPHS SHOWING LATE FRACTURES
AND DEFORMED ZONED PLAGIOCLASE

PUTMAN AND ALFORS, PLATE 2
The Geological Society of America Special Paper 119

section as multiple stages of fracturing and deformation of individual mineral grains which occurred as a result of simultaneous crystallization and continuing magma movement (Pl. 2, fig. 2). Locally, protoclastic deformation is visible on a megascopic scale. Crude foliation is present locally at the contacts and in a few interior outcrops (vicinity 5N-4E), and is presumably a result of slight movement in largely crystallized rock. Shear fractures, which parallel the contact (vicinity 4N-9E), and intersecting slickensided surfaces (vicinity 5N-8W) appear to be deformation features in the margins of the stock which developed as a result of continued rise of magma in the interior. Locally, fractures appear to have developed in several stages late in the consolidation of the rock mass in which they occur. In a riprap quarry at locality 7N-8W, a fracture exhibiting "slickensided" ferromagnesian minerals appears to be truncated by a 1-foot-thick aplite dike. A series of heavily limonite-stained fractures with little, if any, visible component of movement are also present in the quarry, and appear to intersect another aplite dike. These latter fractures carry abundant pyrite and thin films of aplite, whereas sulfides are rare in most of the well-defined aplite dikes. Other structural elements sometimes found in granitic rocks such as schlieren, inclusion swarms, mineralogical layering or banding, multiple shear zones (MacColl, 1964), planar flow structures, and intrusion breccia are not present in the Rocky Hill stock.

WALL ROCKS OF THE STOCK

Serpentinite and regionally metamorphosed serpentinite constitute most of the exposed wall rocks of the stock; only small portions of the exposed contact are with metavolcanic rocks and metagabbro. The ultramafic belt which flanks Rocky Hill extends southeastward into the Lindsay and Frazer Valley quadrangles, and is part of an even larger belt of ultramafic rocks which extends beyond the limits of Figure 1. The serpentinite of the Rocky Hill belt has been metamorphosed, perhaps to the same degree as associated metagabbros, metavolcanics, and metasedimentary rocks. Local variants in the serpentinite include talc schist, relict dunite, tremolite-actinolite rocks, and, at Lewis Hill north of Porterville, a large breccia mass with carbonate matrix.

Metavolcanic rocks (mainly amphibolite) and metasedimentary rocks in the Rocky Hill area were described by Durrell (1940) and included in his Kaweah Series. To the southeast of Rocky Hill, the metavolcanic rocks rapidly decrease in outcrop area, and metasedimentary rocks of a sequence containing metachert, quartzite, slate, phyllite, recrystallized limestone, and quartz-mica schist become much more abundant.

Metagabbro tends to occur in massive, relatively resistant block outcrops which stand above the adjacent ultramafic rocks, and provide abundant talus and surficial debris. In many areas, metagabbro outcrops too small to show on Figures 1 and 2 are completely enclosed and surrounded by serpentinite. Durrell (1940) interpreted the metagabbro as being sills in the serpentinite with considerable lateral continuity. Except for relatively large and very coarse-grained units which may be remnants of once larger bodies, such as that directly south-southeast of Rocky Hill, most of the metagabbro in serpentinite appears to be tectonically distributed blocks of various sizes.

In a previous paper (Putman and Alfors, 1965), it was implied that tremolite in a metachert block in serpentinite (dated at 307 [±30] m.y.) developed as a result of intrusion of an ultramafic mass which is now serpentinized. We feel this view is no longer tenable because the serpentinite itself has been metamorphosed, and we suggest that the age represents regional metamorphism of the country rocks (Kaweah Series). It is possible that the metamorphism was coincident with tectonic emplacement and serpentinization of the ultramafic rocks prior to emplacement of the Rocky Hill stock.

Locally, at the contacts of the stock, both wall rocks and granodiorite are foliated and sheared parallel to the contact. These effects appear to be due to cataclasis and recrystallization in the contact rocks accompanying internal movements in the stock after the margin crystallized. However, the lack of consistently recognized planar or foliate structural elements elsewhere in the wall rocks precludes a determination of the nature of their structural deformation during the initial emplacement of the magma. Protoclastic shear in the granodiorite indicates that some element of forceful intrusion was present, but the extent of deformation in the ultramafic rocks is unknown. In view of the previous tectonic history of this rock unit, detailed structural fabric studies in the area surrounding the stock are probably not warranted.

Petrography, Mineralogy, and Analyses

PETROGRAPHY OF THE GRANODIORITE

The rim-facies granodiorite is a massive, medium-grained hypidio-morphic-granular rock composed of zoned plagioclase, quartz, perthitic potassium feldspar, biotite, hornblende, rare pyroxene, and accessory magnetite, sphene, apatite, zircon, pyrite, pyrrhotite, ilmenite, and allanite (Pl. 1, fig. 1). It is light gray due largely to the white feldspars and gray quartz. The average grain size is 3 to 4 mm, but some grains of potassium feldspar and plagioclase are up to 10 mm or more long. Plagioclase and quartz tend to form mono-mineralic aggregates of grains up to 15 mm in length. The hornblende and, to a lesser extent, the biotite tend to aggregate into erratically distributed clots. Rare pyroxene grains are rimmed by hornblende. Biotite occurs as individual grains up to 3 mm in diameter, as aggregates to 5 mm, and as marginal growths around hornblende clots.

The core-facies granodiorite is composed of the same minerals as the rim-facies but is texturally different. Typical core-facies rocks are characterized by an inequigranular or somewhat porphyritic texture in which 55 to 60 percent of the rock consists of zoned plagioclase which averages 2 to 3 mm long, slightly smaller ovoid or subhedral quartz, and ferromagnesian minerals. The remainder of the rock is a fine- to very fine-grained matrix of potassium feldspar, quartz, and albite (Pl. 1, fig. 2). Potassium feldspar grains larger than 0.5 mm are rare. In general, rocks with more than 20 percent matrix and few or no potassium feldspar grains larger than 0.5 mm are classified here as core-facies granodiorite, although some core-facies rocks mapped in Figure 2 have only 10 percent matrix. The distinction in these latter cases is based mainly on texture and grain size and lack of coarse-grained potassium feldspar. The core-facies granodiorite grades into the rim-facies granodiorite by a decrease in the amount of matrix and increase in the amount of coarse-grained potassium feldspar.

19

Both core- and rim-facies granodiorite contain deformed and broken mineral grains, but in general the deformation is more severe in rim-facies rocks. A somewhat subjective plot of the intensity of protoclastic deformation using as criteria (1) the number of fractured grains of plagioclase, potassium feldspar and quartz, (2) the extent of separation and rotation of the broken fragments, (3) the number of bent glide twin lamellae in plagioclase, (4) the severity of the undulose extinction and recrystallization in quartz, and (5) the number of bent biotite grains as shown in Figure 4. Some of the fractures, especially in the plagioclase (Pl. 2, fig. 2), are healed by quartz, sodic plagioclase, and potassium feldspar, but other fractures are open or are filled by calcite possibly derived through surface weathering. The fractures in some grains do not penetrate adjoining grains and are of protoclastic origin, but the late unfilled fractures especially visible in the quartz grains (Pl. 2, fig. 1) have a definite orientation which parallels the planar grain fractures observed in outcrop. Protoclastic deformation began long before crystallization was complete, as is shown especially by multiple fracturing seen in the plagioclase, and continued until the rock was essentially solid—at least in the rim-facies. Protoclastic deformation is not noted in the aplites and is of diminished in-

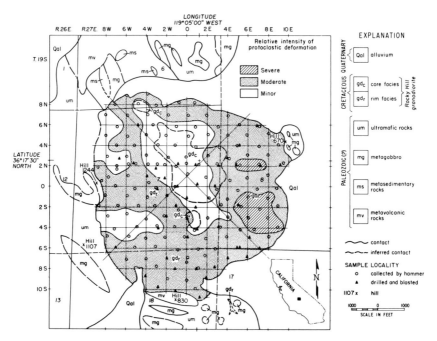

Figure 4. Plot of the relative intensity of protoclastic deformation in the Rocky Hill stock.

tensity in the core-facies rocks, a fact which may be attributed to the cushioning effect of the liquid remaining in the last stages of consolidation when differential vertical movements within the stock have ceased. The differences in intensity between the zones of deformation shown in Figure 4 are small, but they are believed to be real.

MINERALOGY

Plagioclase

Plagioclase grains in the rim-facies rocks are subhedral to euhedral and average 3 to 4 mm long. The core-facies plagioclase commonly tends to be more euhedral and averages 2 to 3 mm long. In both facies, plagioclase grains commonly aggregate into glomeroporphyritic groups which have a common zoning. The boundaries of the individual grains are euhedral or subhedral, except in contact with other grains in the coalescent group. Vance (1957, p. 1849) has stated that the contrast between the euhedral zones and outer boundaries of the coalescent grains and their irregular mutual boundaries is compatible only with crystallization from a magma.

Most plagioclase compositions were determined by universal stage using the curves for plutonic plagioclase given by Slemmons (1962). Supplemental determinations were made from extinction angles on grains oriented by the universal stage so that the a-crystallographic axes were vertical (Deer and others, 1963b, Fig. 55, p. 138).

Plagioclase crystals from both rim- and core-facies granodiorite are strongly zoned from calcic andesine to sodic oligoclase. The most anorthitic cores measured in rim-facies plagioclase are An_{46} and in core-facies plagioclase An_{47}. Margins of rim-facies plagioclase commonly are An_{12}, and a margin as sodic as An_8 was noted on one grain. The most sodic margins measured in core-facies plagioclase phenocrysts are An_{11}.

Oscillatory-normal zoning occurs in plagioclase from both facies, but it is best developed in plagioclase of the core-facies and transitional granodiorite. Many of the grains measured in both rim- and core-facies granodiorite showed a normal zoning with only minor oscillations from An_{47} to $An_{27 \pm 3}$, then an abrupt change in composition to $An_{20 \pm 2}$. After this abrupt change the rim-facies plagioclase generally were normally zoned to $An_{14 \pm 12}$ at the margin. In granodiorite of the core-facies, plagioclase grains very commonly have a broad zone in which the composition oscillates around An_{21} and then is normally zoned to $An_{17 \pm 11}$ at the margin. A zone of muscovite, calcite, and very small unknown inclusions commonly occurs in core-facies plagioclase near the boundary of the last An_{20} zone. Figure 5 shows the distribution of

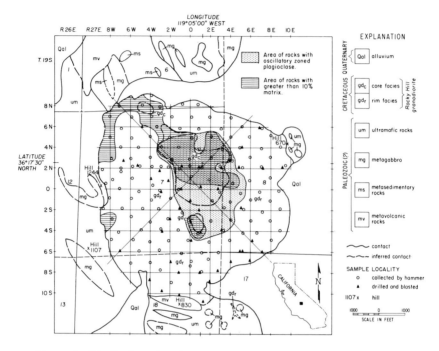

Figure 5. Distribution of rocks containing plagioclase with a broad reversal zone near the grain margins, and rocks with greater than 10 percent fine-grained matrix.

samples which contain numerous plagioclase grains with such a broad zone of composition reversal close to the margin of the grains. Plagioclase grains within a thin section have grossly similar zoning patterns, but even at this scale significant differences have been noted in the sequence and composition of zones between individual grains.

Plagioclase grains of both rock facies commonly have cores showing resorption effects (Pl. 2, fig. 2). Twinning is abundant in the plagioclase grains of both facies of granodiorite. The most common twin laws in order of abundance are: albite, Carlsbad, albite-Carlsbad, and pericline. Pericline twins occur in the calcic portions of the grains; none were observed in the sodic margins. Pericline twinning appears to have formed earlier than much of the albite twinning, and is partially obliterated by albite twinning. Carlsbad twins are probably growth twins, but most of the albite and perhaps the pericline twins as well appear to be deformation or glide twins (Vance, 1961, p. 1103). Albite twinning, especially, can be related to deformation in plagioclase crystals, and is usually most abundant in grains which are severely bent or broken.

In other grains, or rarely even in the same grains, primary albite twinning appears to be present. Primary albite twinning is best shown in the less deformed grains, but even in moderately deformed grains primary albite twinning can still be recognized (Vance, 1961, p. 1103).

The calcic cores of many plagioclase crystals contain swarms of opaque needle-like inclusions up to 0.1 mm in length which produce a clouded appearance in the central portions of the grains. Commonly these inclusions are aligned in three or four sets which intersect the albite twin planes. The quantity of opaque needles is not uniform within a thin section, as some plagioclase grains contain few or none, whereas other grains contain a large number. Except for deuteric alteration, the sodic rims of the plagioclase are clear. Poldervaart and Gilkey (1954) have reviewed the various theories of clouded plagioclase with the conclusion that slight clouding is probably due to exsolution of iron present in the feldspar lattice at the time of its formation. More intense clouding is believed to be the result of the migration of iron and other elements into the crystal after its formation. One or both of these mechanisms may have been involved in producing the needle-like inclusions of the Rocky Hill plagioclase, but the variability in quantity and the restriction of the clouding to the cores of the grains suggests a relict distribution in calcic plagioclase grains dating from the time of magma formation. Electron microprobe traverses show that the needle-like inclusions contain abundant iron and no calcium or titanium, so they are probably magnetite.

Quartz

Quartz on both the rim- and core-facies shows a tendency to form euhedral or subhedral grains, although anhedral grains are most abundant. Some grains in the rim-facies and phenocrysts in the core-facies are well-formed bipyramidal crystals with only short prism faces or none at all. Resorption and modification of the margins of the grains is evident in many quartz grains. Individual grains average 2 or 3 mm in diameter, but commonly aggregate into larger patches. Nearly all the grains show undulose extinction, and some grains which are highly deformed have recrystallized into a number of subindividuals.

Potassium Feldspar

Potassium feldspar generally forms anhedral grains which are interstitial to quartz and plagioclase. Larger grains are zoned and the subhedral central zones are made visible in sawed slabs by staining with potassium rhodizonate without a $BaCl_2$ dip. The early-crystallized central areas of the grains are more deeply stained because of relatively high barium and strontium contents (approximately 1000 and 200 ppm respectively as determined by X-ray spectroscopy).

Microcline grid twinning is visible in many of the potassium feldspar grains, but X-ray diffractometer patterns made by H. Seck (1966, written commun.) shows no splitting of the (131) reflection. Coatney (1965, p. 85-86) has observed the same phenomenon in potassium feldspar from the northern Sierra Nevada and suggests that the Δ—value ($\Delta = 12.5 \, [d_{131} - d_{1\bar{3}1}]$) in triclinic potassium feldspar with unresolved peaks is probably not greater than 0.2. Coatney used the term "minimum microcline" for potassium feldspar with grid twinning but with a Δ—value near orthoclase. Some doubt exists, however, at the present time as to the effectiveness of the (131) method alone as a structural indicator in potassium feldspar with small Δ—value (D. O. Emerson, 1966, oral commun.).

Most of the larger potassium feldspar grains are perthitic, and the size and texture of the exsolved albite lamellae are quite variable. The indicated composition of albite lamellae large enough for extinction angle measurements is about An_6.

No optical or X-ray diffraction determinations of the composition of the potassium feldspar were made, but a partial X-ray spectroscopic analysis gave a value of 12.5 ± 1 percent K_2O. This, combined with the anorthite content of the albite lamellae, would indicate a bulk composition of roughly $Or_{75}Ab_{23}An_2$ for the perthitic potassium feldspar.

Hornblende

Hornblende occurs as individual grains up to 4 mm long, but more commonly forms aggregates of grains up to 5 mm across. Some grains are twinned on (100) and many contain inclusions of quartz, plagioclase, magnetite, apatite, and sphene. Rims of biotite about hornblende grains and aggregates are common. Much of the hornblende, especially in the rim-facies granodiorite, is zoned with a pale-colored core and a highly colored rim. The range in pleochroism is: X = colorless to yellow; Y = very pale green to dark greenish-brown; Z = very pale green to dark olive- or blue-green. Universal stage measurements of 2V and extinction angles on a number of twinned hornblende grains were: $Z \wedge c = 14° - 18°$, $2V_x = 50° - 82°$. The more highly colored grains or zones generally have lower 2V's and extinction angles.

The ratio 100 Mg: $(Mg + Fe^{+2} + Fe^{+3})$ in three analyzed samples of hornblende from the Rocky Hill granodiorite ranged from 39 (highly colored) to 55 (light colored). Neglecting Mn content, ratio values of 39 to 55 for the Rocky Hill hornblende would correspond to a $2V\alpha$ of 62° and 73° respectively on the plot given by Deer and others, (1963a, Fig. 76, p. 296). Agreement between these values and the measured $2V_x$ range of 50° to 82° for the Rocky Hill hornblende appears satisfactory considering the standard deviation of the $2V\alpha$ plot and the fact that neither the most magnesian nor the most iron-rich hornblende from the Rocky Hill granodiorite was chemically analyzed.

Pyroxene

Pyroxene is rare in both core- and rim-facies granodiorite, but less so in the rim-facies. Less than 10 percent of the thin sections studied contained pyroxene and no thin section contained more than three grains. All of the pyroxene occurs in the cores of hornblende grains and in topotactic relation to the hornblende. Many grains contain inclusions of magnetite, apatite, and tiny specks of an unidentified highly birefringent mineral. Pyroxene cores range in size from 0.2 mm to 2 mm and are colorless or very pale green with the following pleochroism: X and Y = colorless, Z = very pale green or colorless. Universal stage measurements of $2V_z$ ranged from 58° to 74°; $Z \wedge c$ ranged between 35° and 37°. The pyroxene is probably a diopside or low iron augite, although no chemical or X-ray studies were made.

Biotite

Biotite is generally interstitial to plagioclase, quartz, and large potassium feldspar grains, and commonly occurs as a late mineral in ferromagnesian clots associated with hornblende, rare pyroxene, apatite, magnetite, and sphene. Pleochroism of the biotite is uniform within grains and does not change discernibly from rim- to core-facies rocks. X is light yellow-brown, and Y and Z are dark greenish-brown or dark reddish-brown. Even in adjoining grains, $2V_x$ ranges from 0° to 15°. Many biotite grains are bent and variation in 2V may be at least partly due to strain.

Biotite grains do not show optical zoning, and electron microprobe traverses across several grains failed to show zoning of Mg, Fe, Ti, Al, or Mn. One complete biotite analysis was made (rim-facies sample 2N-7W) and is given in Table 1. Although no complete analysis of core-facies biotite is available for comparison, Rb_2O/K_2O ratios and fluorine contents of a number of essentially pure biotite samples from both core- and rim-facies rocks were determined (Table 2). Absolute values for Rb_2O are not known because of a lack of adequate standards, but, to a first approximation, rim-facies biotite contains less than 300 ppm Rb_2O and core-facies biotite more than 300 ppm Rb_2O.

Accessory Minerals

Magnetite is modally one of the most variable accessory minerals (Fig. 6). Some samples contain no magnetite; others contain 1.12 percent by weight (0.57 percent by volume). Magnetite content of all samples was determined by magnetic susceptibility measurements as described in Appendix I.

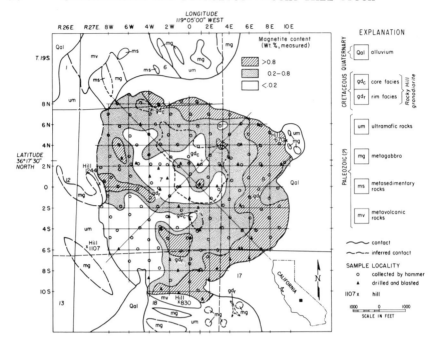

Figure 6. Magnetite distribution in the Rocky Hill stock.

The magnetite content of the 32 modally analyzed samples ranged from 0 to 0.53 percent by volume, and compares favorably with the range of contents indicated by magnetic susceptibility determinations. Magnetite occurs as isolated grains up to 3 mm long and as tiny inclusions in almost all other minerals. Granules of secondary magnetite occur along cleavages in some chloritized biotite and around the borders of some biotite grains. Many of the magnetite grains have a corona of tiny granular sphene which probably developed during late-stage deuteric recrystallization of the magnetite with exsolution of titanium. Electron probe microanalyses show that the magnetite now has virtually no titanium and is thus no longer suitable as a geothermometer. Apatite is a common inclusion in magnetite.

A small amount of ilmenite occurs in some samples and has been verified by X-ray diffraction. Ilmenite occurs in samples with low as well as high magnetite content.

Sphene is a common accessory mineral in both rock facies, but larger grains (maximum 2.5 mm) generally occur in the rim-facies granodiorite. The content of sphene in the samples, as determined by point counting stained slabs, ranged up to 0.4 percent by volume and averages 0.15 percent. The values are low because only larger grains could be counted, but the maximum sphene content probably is about 0.5 percent. Sphene occurs as individual euhedral to anhedral grains and as aggregates of grains associated with ferromagnesian clots. In addition, aggregates of finer-grained sphene rim magnetite and ilmenite grains, and are common in chloritized biotite. Inclusions in sphene include zircon, apatite, and magnetite. In hand specimen the sphene is orange-brown, but in thin section it is nearly colorless and only faintly pleochroic. Two grains measured with a universal stage gave $2V_z$ values of $25°$ and $31°$.

Apatite is a common accessory mineral in all samples. It generally occurs as colorless elongate euhedral pisms and attains a maximum length of 1.5 mm. Apatite typically occurs as inclusions in ferromagnesian minerals and less commonly in plagioclase, quartz, sphene, and potassium feldspar. The content of apatite in the granodiorite as determined by point counting ranged to a maximum of 0.2 percent by volume. This value is possibly low because only larger grains could be counted, but the mean apatite content is probably nearer 0.1 percent. The refractive index, ω, is $1.635 \pm .003$, which

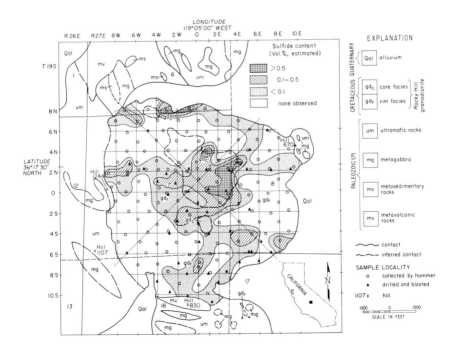

Figure 7. Sulfide distribution in the Rocky Hill stock.

corresponds to 90 mol percent or more fluorapatite (Deer and others, 1962b, Fig. 59, p. 331). The high fluorine content has been confirmed by electron microprobe analysis of an apatite inclusion in biotite.

Zircon is a minor accessory mineral in the Rocky Hill stock and invariably occurs as tiny, colorless euhedral crystals with an average grain size of about 0.05 mm. It most commonly occurs as inclusions in biotite, some of which have pleochroic halos, but is also found in plagioclase, quartz, and allanite.

Allanite is a widely distributed but minor constitutent in the Rocky Hill granodiorite, with an average grain size of about 0.2 mm. It is black in hand specimen and pleochroic from light brown (X') to dark reddish-brown or nearly black (Z') in thin section. Birefringence is moderate and the $2V_x$ is less than 20°; some grains are nearly uniaxial.

The sulfides which occur as accessory minerals in the Rocky Hill granodiorite are pyrite, pyrrhotite, molybdenite, chalcopyrite, and marcasite. Sulfides occur in both facies but are much more abundant in the core-facies rocks (Fig. 7). The data for Figure 7 were determined by binocular inspection of sawed slabs supplemented by observation of weathered sulfides in outcrops. Pyrite, the most abundant and most widespread sulfide in both rock facies, also occurs in aplites, on slickensided fracture surfaces, and along late fractures cutting aplites and rim-facies granodiorite. Pyrrhotite occurs sporadically in some rim-facies rocks and in rocks transitional to the core-facies, especially on the east side of the stock. It has not been identified in the core-facies rocks or in the aplites. Black, sooty, supergene marcasite forms replacement rims on pyrrhotite. Chalcopyrite is a relatively rare constitutent of both rock facies and some aplites. Only in sample O-3E is it relatively abundant. Molybdenite was found only in the sulfide-rich sample, O-3E, and in adjacent aplites. The sulfides are generally late and occupy veinlets and interstices between feldspar and ferromagnesian grains along with fine-grained quartz, chlorite, muscovite, and minor calcite. Pyrrhotite from locality O-3E, heated to restore the hexagonal form, had a d_{102} value of 2.0628 (calibrated with NaCl) which corresponds to 0.937 mol percent FeS and an estimated temperature of formation of 450°C (Toulmin and Barton, 1964, Figs. 2 and 10). Co-existence with pyrite was assumed, and the effect of confining pressure was neglected in this estimate.

Deuteric Effects

Mild deuteric alteration has chloritized some biotite and developed epidote, sericite, and calcite in the cores of many plagioclase grains in both rock facies. The degree of chloritization, however, is greater in the core-facies granodiorite (Fig. 8) as determined from grain counts of chlorite in the ferro-

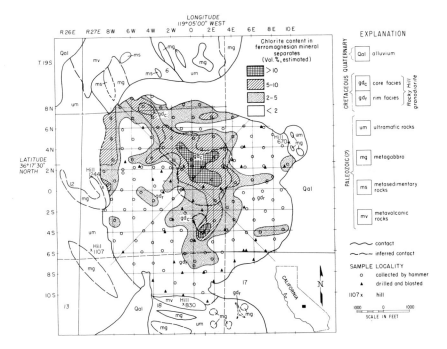

Figure 8. Chlorite distribution in the Rocky Hill stock.

magnesian separates. Deuteric alteration is erratic with scattered grains of chloritized or partially chloritized biotite surrounded by unaltered biotite. Development of sericite and epidote in plagioclase grains is similarly sporadic with intensely altered grains adjoining slightly sericitized and epidotized plagioclase. Epidote also occurs in unchloritized ferromagnesian clots, and it is possible that crystallization of some epidote is related to a late magmatic rather than an exclusively post-magmatic deuteric stage. Some aplite dikes also contain clots of epidote up to 2 inches long. Core-facies rocks contain individual grains of muscovite up to 0.5 mm in altered plagioclase cores and as a constituent of the matrix, but most muscovite is very fine-grained. Some calcite occurs in monomineralic veinlets, and is probably related to surface weathering rather than deuteric alteration.

Paragenesis

The crystallization sequence (Fig. 9) for minerals in the Rocky Hill granodiorite has been deduced in large part from textural relations, especially the relation of inclusions to host mineral and the presence of overgrowths. Plagioclase is a particularly useful mineral because inclusions can be related to the anorthite content of the zone in which they appear, and thus to the stage of crystallization at a particular locality. The accessory minerals, magnetite, apatite, sphene, and zircon, appear to be the first minerals to begin crystallizing. Magnetite and apatite especially occur as inclusions in the calcic portions of plagioclase grains. The mutual relations of grains in ferromagnesian clots indicate that pyroxene began crystallizing first, and was followed by hornblende and then biotite. It is possible that crystallization of pyroxene preceded that of plagioclase, although this is not considered likely because of the low total ferromagnesian content and the fact that no pyroxene inclusions were noted in plagioclase. Quartz began to crystallize early as shown by inclusions in calcic plagioclase and in hornblende grains. The subhedral bipyramidal quartz crystals also tend to indicate early crystallization. Hornblende probably started to crystallize shortly after quartz; hornblende inclusions do not

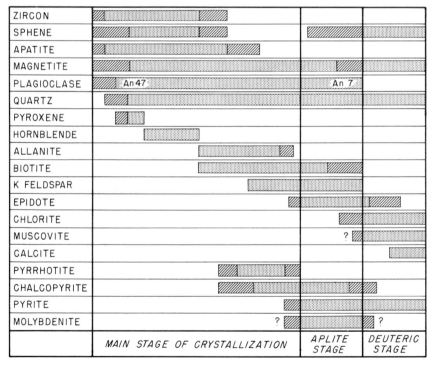

NOTE: The length of the bar does not designate the duration of crystallization or the quantity of material crystallized, only the relative time of crystallization.
= Questionable

Figure 9. Generalized paragenetic sequence of the minerals in the Rocky Hill stock.

occur in the most calcic or most sodic portions of plagioclase grains. Biotite began to crystallize after hornblende, and it occurs as marginal grains around hornblende. Biotite occurs as inclusions in the sodic portions of plagioclase and also projects into some quartz grains. Fine-grained shreds of biotite occur in the matrix of core-facies rocks and also in the aplites. Late crystallizing biotite is found along shear surfaces where it is commonly aligned and smeared out. Potassium feldspar was one of the last minerals to start crystallizing. It commonly occurs as anhedral grains which are interstitial to the other minerals and as a prominent constituent of the matrix of core-facies rocks. The subhedral cores of some zoned potassium feldspar grains indicate, however, that the crystals apparently grew unhindered for a short duration during their paragenesis.

The sulfides—pyrrhotite, pyrite, chalcopyrite, and molybdenite—are generally late and in part are contemporaneous with the deuteric stage. Pyrrhotite and chalcopyrite appear to be the earliest sulfides to crystallize and were followed by pyrite and possibly molybdenite.

Miscellaneous Rocks

A number of other rocks in addition to the rim- and core-facies granodiorite occur in the Rocky Hill stock. These include aplites and associated pegmatites, various kinds of inclusions, "pseudodikes" near 3S-6W, and apophyses and dykes into the country rock.

Aplites. The aplites are fine-grained allotriomorphic granular rocks composed of quartz, unzoned albite, perthitic potassium feldspar, and minor accessory minerals. Chemical and modal analyses of some Rocky Hill aplite samples are given by Putman and Alfors (1965, Table 1, p. 361). The average grain size of the aplites varies from 0.05 mm to 0.5 mm. Some aplites also contain pegmatitic zones with grains several inches long. The grain size of an individual aplite is generally fairly uniform, but some contain phenocrysts of zoned plagioclase, quartz, and even potassium feldspar. Plagioclase phenocrysts occur as large subhedral zoned crystals up to 5 mm long, and as coalescent aggregates of grains to 5 mm. The cores of zoned phenocrysts are as calcic as An_{35}; the rims are as sodic as An_7. Some potassium feldspar phenocrysts are up to 4 mm; most are perthitic and a few contain euhedral quartz inclusions. Individual quartz grains are up to 2 mm with aggregates to 8 mm. These larger feldspar and quartz grains in the aplites are probably "xenocryst" inclusions which have been derived from the parent granodiorite in the process of injection. Deuteric alteration, especially muscovitization, is present to a greater or lesser degree, usually in direct proportion to the thickness of the dike.

Pseudodike rock. The "pseudodikes" in the vicinity of 3S-6W are medium-grained allotriomorphic granular rocks composed of approximately 45 percent quartz, 45 percent plagioclase, and 10 percent ferromagnesian and accessory minerals. Anhedral strained quartz grains form aggregates to 15 mm with individual grains to 4 mm. Two generations of plagioclase are present in these rocks—the older is bytownite with a composition of $An_{86 \pm 3}$ and the younger is andesine with a composition of $An_{43 \pm 5}$. The bytownite is partially replaced by quartz, andesine, and clinozoisite. Quartz is the main replacement mineral with andesine next in abundance and clinozoisite minor. Actinolitic amphibole, much of it occurring as acicular aggregates, constitutes about 5 percent of the rock. Accessory minerals are sphene, ilmenite, allanite, apatite, and rare zircon.

The paragenesis of the pseudodike rock appears to involve the following events. First, potassium feldspar and zoned plagioclase in the original granodiorite were replaced by bytownite with the loss of potassium and sodium, and the ferromagnesian minerals replaced by actinolite, again with loss of alkalis. Later the bytownite was partially replaced by quartz, andesine, and clinozoisite. Boundaries of the pseudodikes with the rim-facies granodiorite are gradational, and these changes vary in intensity accordingly. A possible mechanism to accomplish this rock conversion must involve a hydrothermal vapor phase alkali leach probably operating through en echelon fractures in the granodiorite. The original fractures are now marked by quartz veins an inch or so wide with the alteration extending up to 5 feet on either side of the veins.

Apophyses and dikes. The larger apophyses are medium-grained and at least superficially resemble the rim-facies granodiorite. Only two dike rocks were sampled, one near 0-9W and the other near 4S-9W; they differ modally, but plagioclase compositions are similar. The dike near 0-9W is about 4 feet thick, and could be traced for about 200 feet. It intrudes metagabbro and ultramafic rock, and has selvages a few inches thick of pink clinozoisite and white diopside. A hand specimen from the center of the dike contains an estimated 25 to 30 percent quartz, 55 to 60 percent plagioclase ($An_{34 \pm 9}$), 10 to 15 percent ferromagnesian (chiefly hornblende) and accessory minerals, and virtually no potassium feldspar.

The dike near 4S-9W is about 2 feet thick and intrudes ultramafic rocks. A thin (⅛ inch) selvage of epidote occurs along the contact. The dike contains an estimated 30 to 35 percent quartz, 50 to 55 percent plagioclase ($An_{38 \pm 20}$), 5 percent potassium feldspar, and 5 to 10 percent ferromagnesian minerals.

Inclusions. Inclusions in the Rocky Hill granodiorite, with the exception of one angular inclusion of amphibolite and one of mica schist, are rounded and generally have the composition of a leucocratic quartz diorite. They are finer-grained, contain less potassium feldspar, and generally have more ferromagnesian minerals than the granodiorite. Most of the inclusions have a uniform grain size which averages between 0.2 and 0.3 mm, but some are slightly porphyritic (or porphyroblastic) with phenocrysts (or porphyroblasts) up to 7 mm long. Most grains are anhedral but much of the plagioclase is subhedral, and some plagioclase and hornblende grains are euhedral. Modes of the inclusions range from 20 to 40 percent quartz, 40 to 55 percent plagioclase, 0 to 5 percent potassium feldspar, and 5 to 10 percent each for hornblende and biotite. Accessory minerals are the same as those in the granodiorite. Most plagioclase grains in the inclusions are zoned (range An_{39} to An_{13}), but the groundmass plagioclase in one porphyritic inclusion is unzoned or only slightly zoned with a composition near An_{20}. Some plagioclase phenocrysts contain tiny opaque needle-like inclusions similar to those observed in some plagioclase grains of the granodiorite.

WALL ROCKS

Ultramafic Rocks

Ultramafic rocks (Fig. 1) include serpentinites, partially serpentinized dunites, tremolite-chlorite, and tremolite-talc rocks. The serpentinites are light to dark green, massive to somewhat foliated, and are derived from dunites and peridotites. They are composed of one or more serpentine-group minerals, magnetite, and chromite. Brucite was not identified in the small number of specimens studied. Antigorite is the most abundant serpentine-group mineral; its identification has been verified by X-ray diffraction. Relict outlines of former pyroxene grains are preserved as areas of antigorite which contain abundant dusty magnetite.

The partially serpentinized dunites are dark green, yellow-brown weathering, massive rocks composed of olivine, "serpentine," clinochlore, and magnetite; anthophyllite, talc, and chromite are present in some specimens. The rocks have an equigranular texture with anhedral grains and cleavage fragments of olivine (0.05 to 0.7 mm in size) separated one from the other by a mantle of light yellow "serpentine" and thin plates of clinochlore. Specimens studied in thin section contain 10 to 60 percent serpentine-group minerals and 25 to 70 percent olivine. Most of the olivine grains contain minute irregularly distributed magnetite inclusions. An average $2V_z$ of $88° \pm 4°$ for the olivine corresponds to a composition of $Fo_{89\pm9}$ (Deer and others, 1962a, Fig. 11, p. 22). The composition determined from the X-ray determinative curve of Hotz and Jackson (1963) is $Fo_{94\pm2}$. Some samples of serpentinized dunite from the contact aureole of the Rocky Hill stock contain scattered, long

(5 mm) prismatic grains of anthophyllite, which are partly serpentinized and chloritized along grain boundaries, fractures, and cleavages. The anthophyllite is colorless and, unlike most of the olivine, is completely free of magnetite inclusions. In addition to dusty magnetite, large scattered grains of magnetite are common and many large grains are rimmed by, or intergrown with, clinochlore. Clinochlore also occurs as large individual plates, fine-grained aggregates, or as plates intergrown with "serpentine" or talc. Talc occurs as irregular veinlets and aggregates, and constitutes up to 10 percent of those specimens in which it occurs. Almost all of the serpentinized dunites contain veinlets of carbonates (mainly magnesite) and chalcedony or quartz.

Tremolite-chlorite rocks are light to dark green, and although some are massive, most have a marked schistosity. These rocks are composed largely of a member of the tremolite-actinolite series, chlorite, and magnetite or chromite, but nearly all specimens examined contain small amounts of relict antigorite. White tremolite, or less commonly green actinolite, is generally the most abundant mineral in these rocks, but some specimens contain up to 55 percent chlorite.

Tremolite-talc rocks are white to pale green, fine-grained, and foliated. They are composed largely of colorless tremolite with smaller amounts of talc and minor amounts of magnetite. A minor amount of a pale green, low birefringent, length-slow platy mineral, which may be relict "serpentine," occurs in isolated aggregates throughout.

Metagabbro

Metagabbro of the Rocky Hill area occurs in a wide variety of textural and mineralogical types. It is typically medium- to coarse-grained, although some portions are pegmatitic with crystals up to 5 or 6 inches long, and other portions are relatively fine-grained and grade into metavolcanic rock. In the field the distinction between metagabbro and metavolcanic rock was based on grain size and fabric, but in some outcrops the grain size is so variable that the classification is quite arbitrary.

Typical metagabbro is massive, white and dark-green spotted, and originally contained approximately equal amounts of plagioclase and mafic minerals. Some metagabbros are foliated or lineated with amphibole prisms and plagioclase grains aligned in parallel orientation. Relict minerals include calcic plagioclase, a clinopyroxene which is probably diopsidic augite ($2V_z = 50\text{-}60°$, $Z\wedge c = 38°$), and magnetite. The relict plagioclase contains veinlets and inclusions of epidote or clinozoisite and calcite, and in some outcrops is replaced by hydrogrossular. Many of the plagioclase grains are granulated and recrystallized. In one specimen the recrystallized plagioclase has a composition of about An_{50}, whereas the relict plagioclase is about An_{90}. Many specimens contain, in addition to relict clinopyroxene, a fine-grained, newly crystallized diopside. Blue-green hornblende, the most common mafic mineral, occurs as large, more or less equant, grains which have probably developed from pyroxene.

Metavolcanic Rocks

Metavolcanic rocks in the Rocky Hill area are quite variable in texture. Some are very fine-grained and still retain relict volcanic structures such as vesicules, whereas others are thoroughly recrystallized into layered and strongly lineated amphibolites. Even adjoining outcrops of metavolcanic rocks, especially those present as tectonic blocks in ultramafic rocks, may be quite different in general appearance. The metavolcanic rocks are generally dark green to black, massive, and composed of blue-green hornblende, plagioclase, clinozoisite, magnetite, and minor quartz. An unusual fine-grained foliated metavolcanic rock which occurs as a one-half-mile-long tectonic block in ultramafic rock 2.5 miles northeast of Lindsay is composed of epidote, chlorite, biotite, and quartz. Other variants include medium- to very coarse-grained amphibole-garnet rocks which occur as tectonic blocks up to 10 feet long in ultramafic rock in NW $\frac{1}{4}$, Sec. 11, T.20 S., R.27 E., M.D.M.

Metasedimentary Rocks

Quartz mica schist, micaceous quartzite, phyllite, and carbonaceous slate comprise the bulk of the metasedimentary rocks in the Rocky Hill area, although metachert, limestone, and dolomitic limestone are also common. Two miles east of Lindsay in SW $\frac{1}{4}$, NW $\frac{1}{4}$, Sec. 10, T.20 S., R.27 E., M.D.M., an uncommon piemontite-bearing quartz muscovite schist occurs as a tectonic block in ultramafic rock. This schist contains about 85 to 90 percent quartz, 5 to 10 percent muscovite, 5 percent piemontite, 1 percent magnetite, and 1 percent garnet. Tectonic blocks of metachert in ultramafic rock commonly contain abundant magnetite and tremolite. An unusual metachert breccia composed of quartz, blue-green amphibole, brown stilpnomelane, and magnetite occurs as a tectonic block in ultramafic rock in the center of S $\frac{1}{2}$, Sec. 28, T. 19 S., R. 27 E., M.D.M.

Contact Metamorphism by the Rocky Hill Stock

Contact metamorphism by the Rocky Hill stock has caused the development of blue-green hornblende, diopside, plagioclase, garnet, epidote, and clinozoisite in the metagabbro and metavolcanic rocks. West of the Rocky Hill stock, between grid points 0-9W and 1S-8W, several granodiorite dikes or apophyses have irregular selvages several inches thick of pink clinozoisite, epidote, brown garnet, white and green diopside, and plagioclase (An_{70} in one specimen).

Durrell (1940, p. 82) states that, in the serpentinites, the outermost limit of contact metamorphism by the stock is about 1000 feet from the contact, and is marked by the appearance of colorless actinolitic hornblende and the replacement of serpentine minerals by clinochlore. According to Durrell (1940, p. 85), olivine, enstatite-hypersthene, green spinel, and tremolite are found only within 100 feet, and commonly only within a few tens of feet of the contact. In the present study, actinolite, tremolite, and clinochlore were found to be common minerals in the metaserpentinites and are not restricted to a metamorphic aureole around the stock. No enstatite-hypersthene was identified in the rocks collected for the present study, but olivine occurs in metaserpentinite samples collected as far as 1.5 miles from the Rocky Hill stock. The olivine in these specimens appears to be relict grains rather than olivine regenerated from serpentine by contact metamorphism as suggested by Durrell (1940, p. 82-88). Anthophyllite apparently is the only mineral which has crystallized in response to contact metamorphism by the Rocky Hill stock that has not been found elsewhere in the metaserpentinites.

The assemblages hornblende-diopside-plagioclase in the mafic rocks and anthophyllite-clinochlore in the ultramafic rocks are typical of the hornblende-hornfels facies of contact metamorphism (Turner and Verhoogen, 1960, p. 514-516). However, except for anthophyllite (which seems restricted to relict dunites among the contact rocks), these minerals also occur in the regional metamorphic terrain. Consequently, a mineralogically well-defined contact aureole is not present, although more subtle effects, such as changes in phase composition, may exist.

SUMMARY OF ANALYTICAL DATA FROM ROCKS AND MINERALS OF THE STOCK

In view of the amount of field, petrographic, and analytical data to be applied toward a synthesis of the emplacement and crystallization history of the Rocky Hill stock, it seems advisable to present first the analytical data in summary fashion with relevant comment. Largely inductive manipulation and interpretation of the data follows in the next section, where a reconstruction of processes is attempted, and it is more convenient there to refer to the appropriate supporting data in various groups. Following the modal analysis data, a brief description of sample preparation methods is included, since the nature of the material analyzed must be considered in evaluating some of the data.

Modal Analyses

Modal analyses were made of 17 rim-facies and 15 core-facies granodiorite samples, selected along the two diagonal lines shown in Figure 2, and from locality 2N-3E. Where two samples were collected at one locality, both were analyzed. Selectively stained slabs with a minimum area of 4000 mm^2 were used, and an average of about 2000 counts were made per side. Both sides of some slabs were counted. Sodium cobaltinitrite and amaranth (Acid Red 27) were used for staining following the technique of Laniz and others (1964), except that a 1:1 mixture of collodion and methyl alcohol was used in place of molten Lakeside to fill the cracks. A grid reproduced on a photographic plate with a spacing of 1.5 mm was affixed to the stained slabs with mineral oil, and grain identifications were made under a binocular microscope. Chlorite was recorded as biotite; sericite and epidote in plagioclase cores were recorded as plagioclase; and albite lamellae in perthitic potassium feldspar was recorded as plagioclase.

The rim-facies granodiorite has a coarseness index (IC) of 27 (Chayes, 1956). The 4000 mm^2 area counted per slab is thus adequate to provide an average analytical error of ≤ 2.0 percent for the major constituents (Chayes, 1956, Fig. 12). Average modal analyses and variability data for the rim- and core-facies granodiorite are presented in Table 1. The within-slab standard deviations were derived from modal counts on hand specimens on which two parallel surfaces were cut approximately 15 mm apart. In the rim-facies

TABLE 1. AVERAGE MODAL ANALYSES AND COMPONENTS OF STANDARD DEVIATION FOR RIM- AND CORE-FACIES GRANODIORITE, ROCKY HILL STOCK, TULARE COUNTY, CALIFORNIA

	Rim-Facies Granodiorite			Core-Facies Granodiorite		
		Standard Deviation			Standard Deviation	
	Mean Volume (%)	Within Slab	Between Rock Samples	Mean Volume (%)	Within Slab	Between Rock Samples
Quartz	30.62	1.49	1.93	32.31	2.15	2.71
Plagioclase	44.23	2.87	2.34	47.20	1.46	2.87
Potassium feldspar	15.60	3.03	1.61	12.56	1.73	2.64
Biotite	6.97	1.43	1.31	6.71	0.40	1.03
Hornblende	2.18	1.19	0.95	0.81	0.15	0.49
Other	0.40	—	—	0.41	—	—
Total	100.00			100.00		
Degrees of freedom	17	4	16	15	5	14

rocks, sporadic distribution of large potassium feldspar grains, clots of ferro-magnesian minerals, and grouping of tabular plagioclase crystals are reflected in estimates of within-rock-slab variation which equal those between rock samples for all minerals except quartz. The lower estimates of variation within the core-facies slabs is interpreted as a result of the more homogeneous nature of the finer-grained matrix in these rocks. Such relatively large within-slab standard deviations for rim-facies rocks indicate that modal variations among these rocks cannot be effectively determined by means of the sampling design used in this study. However, differences in mean values between the rim- and core-facies rocks appear to be significant for all minerals except biotite and possibly quartz.[2] A QPK diagram of the rim- and core-facies granodiorites (Fig. 10) shows a distinct difference in the two facies based on the amount of potassium feldspar. In contrast, the QMF diagram (Fig. 10) shows considerable overlap of the two facies, especially in total feldspar content, but the samples of core-facies granodiorite do cluster about higher quartz values and the rim-facies granodiorite about higher mafic values.

Sample Preparation Methods

A hand specimen was selected from each sample and approximately 2 kg of the remaining rock material was put through a jaw crusher. About 200 grams were split out in a riffle splitter and pulverized between ceramic plates. Another split of the jaw-crushed material was prepared for use in magnetic susceptibility determinations. Splits of pulverized rock were option-ally made for chemical analyses. The pulverized material was sieved, and the portion between 80 and 150 mesh was used for mineral separations. From this portion, which amounted to about 100 grams for most samples, the mag-netite and scrap iron were removed, and the ferromagnesian minerals (and sphene in some samples) concentrated with a magnetic separator. The ferro-magnesian concentrate was then centrifuged in tetrabromoethane and inspected under a binocular microscope for impurities. Purified concentrates weighed about 5 grams each, and all contained at least 70 percent biotite, with an average content of 85 to 90 percent. The total amount of biotite, hornblende, and chlorite in nearly all ferromagnesian separates exceeded 98 percent. Principal impurities were quartz and feldspar, but very small amounts of apa-tite, zircon, sphene, epidote, allanite, and sulfides persist as inclusions in the ferromagnesian minerals or as composite grains. Similarly purified concen-trates of magnetite and sphene were obtained from most of the samples which were modally analyzed, and potassium feldspar concentrates were separated

---

[2]Potassium feldspar, plagioclase, and hornblende exceed 99 percent confidence limits in t test, and quartz exceeds 90 percent.

from eight samples. Other mineral separates prepared for spectrochemical analysis included three of hornblende, two each of allanite and chlorite, and one sample each of marcasite and chalcopyrite. One concentrate of pyrrhotite used for thermal treatment and subsequent X-ray diffraction study was also prepared.

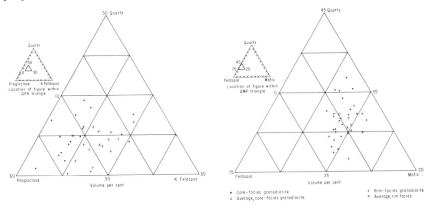

Figure 10. QPK and QMF diagrams of the core- and rim-facies granodiorite, Rocky Hill stock.

Prior to analysis, the ferromagnesian separates were intermittently agitated in 1 N. HCl for five minutes to remove physical metallic contamination. The copper alloy chute of the magnetic separator was coated with an acrylic spray to prevent copper contamination through abrasion during mineral concentration. Minute inclusions of chalcopyrite provided some copper contamination in a few of the mineral separates. Magnetite separates were leached for five minutes or longer in 1 N. HNO_3 to remove scrap iron contamination derived from the jaw-crusher and hammer. All acid-immersed mineral separates were washed subsequently for 10 minutes in distilled water and dried at 80°C before analysis.

All mineral separates and some bulk-rock samples (mainly of inclusions and wall rocks) were analyzed for trace elements and Fe and Mg by d.c. arc emission spectroscopy. Further details of the chemical analysis and physical measurement procedures used in this study, and estimates of their precision, are included in the appendix.

Chemical Analyses of Major Constituents

Essentially complete analyses of composite rim- and core-facies rock samples, one individual rim-facies sample (2N-7W), and the biotite from this sample are shown in Table 2. The composite rock samples were

Table 2. Chemical Analyses of Granodiorite and Biotite, Rocky Hill Stock, Tulare County, California

	Composite Rim-Facies Granodiorite	Composite Core-Facies Granodiorite	Granodiorite 2N-7W	Biotite 2N-7W
SiO_2	71.0	71.5	71.5[1]	37.2[1]
TiO_2	0.54	0.44	0.50	2.60
Al_2O_3	14.2	14.4	14.7	13.3
Fe_2O_3	0.83	0.74	0.67	4.3
FeO	1.85	1.71	1.94	19.4
MnO	.055	.053	0.05	0.45
MgO	0.73	0.74	0.70	8.4
CaO	2.60	2.5	2.5	0.30
Na_2O	4.35	4.3	4.15	0.22[2]
K_2O	3.06	2.77	2.83	9.2[2]
H_2O+[3]	0.76	0.80	0.30	3.19
F	0.06[4]	0.07[4]	0.07[4]	0.90
Less $O \equiv F$	−0.025	−0.03	−0.03	−0.38 $O \equiv F$
Σ Traces[5]				0.52
Totals	100.01	99.99	99.88	99.80

Norms[6]

			Calculated atomic ratio on basis of 24(O, OH, F)[7]	
Q	28.4	31.2	Si	5.77 } 8.00
Or	14.4	12.6	Al	2.23
Ab	36.4	37.0	Al	0.24
An	10.5	10.0	Ti	0.30
Σ others	10.3	9.2	$Fe+^3$	0.50
			$Fe+^2$	2.52 } 5.59
			Mn	0.06
			Mg	1.95
			X[8]	0.02
			Ca	0.02
			Na	0.07 } 1.92
			K	1.82
			Rb	0.00
			Ba	0.01
			OH	3.30 } 3.74 } 24.00
			F	0.44
			O	20.26

[1] SiO_2 by wet chemistry, analyst M. Tavela

[2] Analysed by flame photometry, analyst M. Tavela

[3] Ignition loss estimate, includes minor CO_2 and S. P_2O_5 (not included) in accessory apatite $<0.05\%$ in granodiorite

[4] Calculated from average fluorine content of ferromagnesian separates, and average mode of composite samples

[5] Ba, Cu, V, Zn, Rb, Li, Sr, Y, Zr, B, P, Ni, Co, Cr as oxides

[6] Chemical analysis compensated for some deuteric alteration. K_2O and CaO in biotite and hornblende not included in computed normative feldspar

[7] Apatite and zircon inclusions have been subtracted:
    a) for apatite, subtract 0.12% P_2O_5, 0.16% CaO, 0.01% F, add 0.005% O
    b) for zircon subtract 0.05% ZrO_2 and 0.02% SiO_2
    c) Cl analysed for by X-ray spectrograph and not detected

[8] X = Cu, V, Zn, Sr, Y, B, Ni, Co, Cr

prepared by combining equal-weight splits of the same samples used for modal analyses.

If the relatively small differences in average modes between the rim- and core-facies rocks are real, then corresponding differences should be observed in bulk-rock analyses of composite samples based on these groups. The differences (Table 2) are small, but correspond very closely to the effects predicted by a comparison of average modes. K_2O and total iron are lower in the core-facies composite sample in agreement with a lower content of potash feldspar and ferromagnesian phases. The expected difference in SiO_2 content calculated from the modes is about 1 percent. Whether, in fact, this difference exists is problematical, since deuteric alteration is more intensive in the core-facies rocks and sericitization, chloritization, and calcitization yield lower SiO_2 and Na_2O values. Keeping this in mind, the calculated norms are in relatively good agreement with the average modes of these rock facies. Chemical and modal analyses and norms for aplites from the Rocky Hill stock have been reported previously (Putman and Alfors, 1965).

Table 3 presents selected analytical data for a number of samples, many of which were also used for the modal analyses discussed previously. The mean values cited in Table 3 for iron and fluorine in the two rock facies are derived from all samples used in the modal analyses, while the Rb_2O/K_2O ratios are derived only from the samples listed. All the core-facies rocks are affected by deuteric chloritization to the extent that chlorite comprises 5 to 20+ percent of the ferromagnesian mineral separate. An analysis of chlorite (sample 4S-1E-2) from a core-facies rock is given in Table 3, and it is evident that a loss of fluorine and TiO_2 is to be expected relative to a nonchloritized phase separate. Accordingly, the mean fluorine contents have been derived from data corrected for the degree of chloritization (Fig. 8). The individual sample fluorine values in Table 3 are from the original uncorrected data.

Biotite concentrates, which were obtained by sliding the ferromagnesian concentrates over sheets of paper to remove the nonplaty minerals, were used for the Rb_2O/K_2O determinations. The K_2O contents for all cited analyses were approximately equivalent, and no correction was applied.

Knowledge of the relative oxidation state of iron in ferromagnesian minerals and its partition between various phases is necessary in order to estimate oxygen fugacity and the degree of oxidation occurring during magmatic crystallization. The results of ferric-ferrous iron determinations on some Rocky Hill rock samples and ferromagnesian separates are shown in Table 3. Considerable care must be exercised in sample preparation to prevent oxidation of iron in ferromagnesian phases, as can be seen in the case of four samples with relatively high Fe_2O_3 (4N-3E, 3S-4W, 2N-3E-2, to a lesser extent 2N-7W in

TABLE 3. SELECTED ANALYTIC DATA FOR RIM- AND CORE-FACIES GRANDIORITE

Sample	Bulk rock Wt. %				Ferromagnesian separate						K-feldspar
	Fe_2O_3	FeO	Magnetite	TiO_2	Fe_2O_3	FeO	$\dfrac{MgO^*}{Fe^\circ}$	F	$\dfrac{Rb_2O}{K_2O} \times 10^{-3}$	Remarks	$\dfrac{Rb_2O}{K_2O} \times 10^{-3}$
Rim-facies granodiorite											
8N-7W	0.81	2.14	0.29	—	3.9	19.5	0.42	0.80	—	95% biotite	
8N-7W	—	—	—	—	5.4	17.4	—	—	—	>90% hornblende concentrate	—
6N-5E	0.76	1.82	0.40	—	3.5	18.2	0.50	1.0	—	—	
4N-3E	0.77	1.75	1.10	—	4.9	17.2	0.50	1.0	—	biotite milled to −200 mesh	—
2N-3W-2			0.02	—	4.1	20.9	0.40	—	—	—	
1N-4W-2			0.06	—	3.5	20.7	0.42	—	—	—	—
3S-4W	0.43	2.36	0.00	—	5.7	20.2	0.38	0.85	—	biotite milled to −200 mesh	—
4S-5W	0.66	1.96	0.01	—	5.6	19.6	0.43	0.70	—	weathered sample	
5S-6W	0.39	2.37	0.06	—	3.5	21.9	0.35	0.80	—	—	
6S-7W	0.51	2.33	0.03	—	3.3	21.0	0.40	0.60	2.95	—	1.10
6S-7E	1.01	1.60	0.98	—	3.8	18.1	0.57	—	3.45	—	1.17
10S-1E	0.91	1.46	1.10	—	3.8	18.5	0.55	—	—	—	—
9N-6W			0.63	—	—	—	0.47	—	2.85	—	0.98
(X̄)	0.83	1.85	—	—	—	—	—	0.82	3.08	—	1.08
Std. dev. (s)								0.13			

TABLE 3 (Continued)

| Sample | Bulk rock Wt. % | | | | Ferromagnesian separate | | | | | | K-feldspar |
	Fe$_2$O$_3$	FeO	Magnetite	TiO$_2$	Fe$_2$O$_3$	FeO	$\dfrac{MgO^*}{Fe^\circ}$	F	$\dfrac{Rb_2O}{K_2O} \times 10^{-3}$	Remarks	$\dfrac{Rb_2O}{K_2O} \times 10^{-3}$
					Core-facies granodiorite						
4N-3W	—	—	0.76	—	3.8	17.6	0.54	0.85	—	—	—
2N-1W-2	—	—	0.62	—	3.5	18.9	0.54	0.75	—	—	—
2N-3E-2	0.32	1.67	0.25	—	4.4	19.04	0.47	0.94	—	biotite milled to −200 mesh	
1N-0	0.76	1.73	0.34	—	3.5	20.1	0.41	0.90	—	biotite, >10% chloritized	
0-1W	0.71	1.92	0.14	—	5.3	18.5	0.49	0.80	3.35	weathered sample	1.23
0-1W-2	0.56	2.00	0.10	—	4.1	19.8	0.50	0.93	3.45	—	—
0-3E-2	0.11	2.14	0.00	—	2.1	20.9	0.45	—	3.88	recrystallized biotite, 10% chloritized, from max. sulfide zone	1.21
0-1E	—	—	0.86	—	3.8	18.5	0.53	1.05	—	—	—
2N-1E-2	0.51	1.96	0.10	—	—	—	0.44	1.0	3.88	—	1.23
3N-4E-2	—	—	0.54	—	—	—	0.48	—	3.78	—	1.23
2S-1E	—	—	0.36	—	—	—	0.48	—	3.32	—	1.37
($\overline{X}$)	0.74	1.71	—	—	—	—	—	0.92	3.65	mean F value corrected for degree of chloritization	1.25
Std. dev.(s)	—	—	—	0.6	0.70	—	—	0.12	—	—	—
4S-1E-2	—	—	—	—	—	25.4	—	0.12	—	chlorite	—

*Determined from emission spectroscopic data, coefficient of variation — 8%

Table 2) which were milled in a dry plastic capsule with a ceramic ball. The remaining ferromagnesian separates were either analyzed without further size reduction, or were ground under xylene. Similar oxidation as a result of the initial stages of weathering of the rock is seen in samples O-1W and 4S-5W, where both the rock and the ferromagnesian separate have a relatively high Fe_2O_3 content. Excluding such cases of oxidation, the Fe_2O_3 content of biotites from Rocky Hill is normally 3.5 to 4.0 weight percent with no apparent relation between Fe_2O_3 content and the amount of co-existing magnetite in the rock, or the rock facies. However, despite the scatter in the Fe_2O_3 analyses, these data suggest that the ratio $Fe^{3+}/Fe°$ is higher in the less ferruginous biotites. The data also clearly indicate that the total iron content of the biotite is directly controlled by the amount of co-existing magnetite. Biotite from rocks with little or no magnetite averages about 21 percent FeO, whereas in rocks with 1 percent or more magnetite, biotite has 18 percent or less FeO. Concomitant with these changes an inverse shift in the MgO content occurs such that the ratio $MgO/Fe°$ averages 0.36 for biotite from rocks with no magnetite and 0.54 or more for biotite from rocks containing 1 percent magnetite. Relative to biotite in the same rock, analyzed hornblende has a higher ratio of Fe_2O_3/FeO, with perhaps a slightly lower total iron content (sample 8N-7W, Table 3). Bias in the analytical data of Table 3 produced by diverse amounts of minor hornblende in the ferromagnesian separates is slight. An opposite effect (lower Fe_2O_3, higher FeO) is produced by the presence of minor chlorite, particularly in core-facies separates.

Trace Element Analyses—A Test for Regional Variation

Analytical and statistical data for trace metal analyses of mineral phase separates are summarized in Table 4. The trace elements were selected on the basis of occurrence in more than one phase in sufficient concentration to be analyzed by emission spectroscopy, and as being representative indicators of fractionation or other processes which may have taken place during crystallization of the stock. Naturally, a number of other trace elements can be detected in any one phase, and other choices might have been equally suitable.

Regional analysis of the trace element data (next section), whereby fractionation trends are extracted, is greatly facilitated if the ferromagnesian separates for all samples are reduced to a common modal basis. Biotite and hornblende constitute a paragenetic series at Rocky Hill, and some biotite replaces hornblende. Modally, hornblende and magnetite vary greatly (each is virtually absent in some samples); hornblende is commonly zoned. It is simpler and probably less biased to consider the ferromagnesian-phase mixture in each rock sample as a single "phase" which is represented here by each ferromagnesian mineral separate (Putman and Alfors, 1967). Also implicit in this

TABLE 4. SUMMARY OF MINOR ELEMENT DATA FOR MINERAL PHASE
SEPARATES FROM THE ROCKY HILL STOCK, TULARE COUNTY, CALIFORNIA

	Element	Analytical precision Ca (%)	Within grid Coefficient of variation Cg (%)	Within pluton Gross coefficient of variation C (%)	Mean content $\bar{x}$ (ppm)	F-ratio* $C^2\text{-}Ca^2$ $\overline{Cg^2\text{-}Ca^2}$
Ferro-	Be	5.0	19.5	35.5	2.35	3.48
magnesian	Cr	4.2	11.8	17.7	31.1	2.44
phase	Cu	2.7	33.2	46.2	105	1.94
	Ni	3.6	8.7	15.0	54.5	3.33
	V	2.2	6.7	11.5	403	3.11
	Y	2.8	28.6	38.7	66.1	1.84
	Zn	4.0	6.77	9.1	440	2.22
	Degrees of freedom		32	150		
Magnetite	Cr		27.0	$\gg$100	445	
	Cu		—	>100	85	
	Ni		—	>100	—	
	V		11.0	31.9	2850	
	Y		—	—	28	
	Zn		—	—	<250	
	Degrees of freedom		4	27		
Sphene	Cr		—	—	<2	
	Mo		19.0	20	36.5	
	Ni		—	—	5	
	Sn		4.8	14.3	317	
	V		9.1	9.8	681	
	Y		16.9	27.4	7170	
	Degrees of freedom		3	30		

*All values determined are significant at the 95% level, F>1.65

approach is the fact that each mineral phase analysis is a composite result derived from many grains in a rock sample where any variations between grains and within-grains (zoning) are averaged out. No estimates of within-rock sample variability from these sources were made in this study, and the within-grid or local variation to be discussed subsequently does not include any component at the rock-sample scale.

The analytical precision (Ca) indicated in Table 4 applies to the mean of duplicate determinations. Duplicate analyses of some magnetite and sphene separates indicated a comparable analytical precision for these minerals. The grand mean element content (x) for ferromagnesian separates is derived from analyses representing all 151 grid localities. Data for magnetite and sphene separates are from the samples used for modal analyses. The total elemental variation among all grid localities is given in Table 4 as the within-pluton gross coefficient of variation $(C = \dfrac{S}{\bar{X}} \cdot 100)$. A pooled estimate of the local or with-in-grid component of variation is given in Table 4 as the within-grid coefficient of variation (Cg). The total variation includes the within-grid component, and is not itself an estimate of regional variability. The F ratio in Table 4 tests the significance of the estimates of total variance against those of within-grid vari-ance after both are corrected for increased dispersion due to analytical error. The ratios are significant in every case, thus indicating that each estimate of total variance contains a true regional component. The local variation at the sample locality, however, contributes a substantial portion of the observed total variability (30 to 59 percent of the total variance), and acts like background "noise" which is superimposed on the regional component. Plots of raw ana-lytical data upon the sample grid can be useful in making visual comparisons of the relationships of various properties, for all the data representing any one grid point are obtained from the same sample. Such plots, however, should not be considered as displays of regional trends, for the data of each grid point

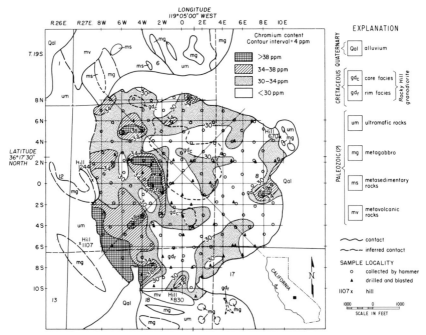

Figure 11.   Chromium in ferromagnesian mineral phases, raw data plot.

are subject to within-grid or local variability as well as to other factors. As an example, a distribution plot based upon the raw results of Cr analyses of all ferromagnesian separates is shown in Figure 11. This plot should be compared to that previously given for magnetite distribution (Fig. 6). The effect of the amount of magnetite in the rock upon the raw Cr distribution plot is easily seen, and a similar situation exists for the other ferro-metals Ni and V, and for Zn.

Variability data for magnetite and sphene obtained from a smaller number of separates are included in Table 4. No test of within-pluton significance was made, but the data serve to illustrate the differences in variability of the same trace element in various phases. A dash in the columns of Table 4 indicates that some analyses of a particular element were near or below the limit of detection, and no estimate of the respective variance was made. The ferromagnesian phase was also analyzed for Ba, but the results are omitted in Table 4 because of sampling bias. Separates from samples obtained by drilling have a higher Ba content than those of the nearest sample collected by hammer in every case. Although no significant difference based on mode of sample collection was indicated for any other element, in the case of Ba the effect is apparently a result of incipient weathering of the outcrop surface.

Additional trace element analytical data for selected mineral phases, wall rocks, inclusions, and bulk granodiorite samples are included in Table 5. This table is intended mainly as a comparison and supplement to Table 4, and is not a list of all trace elements detected in these rock samples or mineral phases.

A few points which emerge from Table 5 perhaps deserve specific comment here. Relative to biotite in the same rock, hornblende usually has a higher content of Be, Cr, and Y, and frequently contains more Ni and less Cu. The higher Cr and Ni contents are in keeping with the earlier paragenesis of hornblende, but the behavior of Be at Rocky Hill is in apparent contrast to the general concepts of its behavior during magmatic crystallization (Rankama and Sahama, 1950; Mason, 1966; Beus, 1962). Since the bulk rock contains roughly the same percentage of Be (mainly in feldspars) as the ferromagnesian phases, only a minor proportion of the total Be in the rock is present in these phases. However, not only does Be tend to be enriched in the earlier ferromagnesian phase (hornblende) in any given rock volume, but Be is depleted in the ferromagnesian phases in the parts of the stock which crystallized last (*see* next section).

An analysis (Table 5) of deuteric chlorite which replaces biotite in a sample of core-facies rock (4S-1E-2) is similar to the average ferromagnesian phase in the contents of trace elements tabulated in Table 4. Consequently, no

TABLE 5. TRACE ELEMENT ANALYSES (PPM) FOR COMPOSITE RIM-
AND CORE-FACIES GRANODIORITE, SELECTED MINERAL
PHASES, INCLUSIONS, AND WALL ROCK SAMPLES

Sample	B*	Be	Cu	Cr	Ni	Mo	Pb*	Sn	V	Zn*	Y
Rim-facies composite	30	1-3	9	n.a.	n.a.	n.d.	5	1.4	n.a.	35	n.a.
Core-facies composite	12	1-3	15	n.a.	n.a.	n.d.	5	1.2	n.a.	30	n.a.
K-feldspar 3N-4E-2	n.d.	n.a.	6	n.d.	n.d.	n.d.	15	1.5	n.d.	15	n.d.
K-feldspar 6S-7E	n.d.	n.a.	9	n.d.	n.d.	n.d.	12	10	n.d.	25	n.d.
Biotite 6S-7E	≃10	3.1	150	29	58	n.d.	14	10	375	450	86
Biotite 6S-5W	n.a.	3.0	78	38	47	n.d.	n.a.	n.a.	470	370	110
Hornblende 6S-5W	n.a.	4.5	44	83	50	n.d.	n.a.	n.a.	430	250	330
Chlorite 4S-1E-2	n.a.	n.d.	57	39	59	n.d.	n.a.	n.a.	390	430	<100
Allanite† 2N-7W	n.a.	n.a.	n.a.	45	46	n.a.	n.a.	150	660	tr.	1800

Sample	Ag	Be	Cu	Cr	Ni	Mo	Sn	V	Zn	Y
Chalcopyrite 0-3E	145	n.d.	xxx	n.d.	45	40	n.d.	21	1650	70
Marcasite 0-3E (pseudomorph after pyrrhotite)	43	1.6	xx	n.d.	275	680	45	18	1170	42
Inclusion vic. 6N-3E	n.d.	1.6	78	23	9	n.d.	n.d.	94	100	31
Inclusion vic. 5N-8E	n.d.	3.0	32	tr.	tr.	n.d.	tr.	39	tr.	19
Inclusion vic. 1S-4E	n.d.	2.2	37	<10	tr.	n.d.	150	39	tr.	7
Inclusion vic. 2S-5W	n.d.	2.5	250	10.5	8.5	n.d.	n.d.	180	130	51
Serpentinite Hill 670	n.d.	n.d.	28	>2000	1100	n.d.	n.d.	46	n.d.	3.5
Serpentinite Hill 1107	n.d.	n.d.	24	≃2000	630	n.d.	n.d.	120	tr.	tr.
Serpentinite Hill 1244	n.d.	n.d.	31	>2000	1250	n.d.	n.d.	110	≃90	5
Metagabbro Hill 670	n.d.	n.d.	34	>2000	255	n.d.	n.d.	135	n.d.	9
Metagabbro Hill 1244	n.d.	n.d.	11	≃1000	265	n.d.	n.d.	135	n.d.	4.5
Metagabbro Hill 830	n.d.	n.d.	8	205	105	n.d.	n.d.	105	n.d.	2
Amphibolite Hill 1244	n.d.	n.d.	68	>2000	380	n.d.	n.d.	150	n.d.	tr.
Amphibolite Hill 830	n.d.	tr.	65	430	130	n.d.	n.d.	210	tr.	17

*Values for boron and lead, and for zinc in granodiorite and K-feldspar are semi-quantitative

†Also present as important minor elements but not determined quantitatively: La, Ce, Yb, Zr, Sm, Co, and Nb. A small amount of Be is present (<10 ppm) but could not be determined because of Ce interference

n.a.=not analyzed

n.d.=not detected

tr.=trace

adjustment was necessary to compensate the ferromagnesian analyses for the degree of chloritization.

A comparison of analyses in Table 5 of the various wall rocks and several typical inclusions in the Rocky Hill rim-facies granodiorite is significant. The inclusions in general now consist of phases similar to those in the granodiorite (zoned plagioclase, quartz, hornblende, biotite, and accessories) but with different textures and modes, and they do not as a group appear to be derived from the presently exposed wall-rock units of serpentinite, metagabbro, and amphibolite. The low Cr and Ni contents of the inclusions could not be produced by assimilation of mafic or ultramafic wall rocks of the pluton without complete loss of textural and modal identity. Inclusions collected near 5N-8E and 1S-4E are more felsic than the others (≈ 10 percent mafics) which is reflected in lower contents of Cr, Ni, V, and Y. The fact that the latter element decreases in the more felsic inclusions is also in distinct contradiction to an origin of most of the inclusions at Rocky Hill by recrystallization or metasomatic reworking of mafic xenoliths from rock types similar to the present wall rocks. Relatively uncommon, and usually rather small, highly mafic inclusions in rim-facies granodiorite were not analyzed in this study and may, however, be derived in the above manner. Textures and modes of typical inclusions together with the analytical data cited above may be more reasonably explained by considering the inclusions as originally derived from rocks similar to the feldspathic quartz-biotite schists which are prominent in exposures of the metasedimentary unit to the southeast of Rocky Hill. However, such rocks were not analyzed in this study.

Specific Gravity Determinations

Results of specific gravity measurements on rim- and core-facies granodiorite from the Rocky Hill stock, and from some of the country rocks of the Rocky Hill area are presented in Table 6. Slight differences in the modal

TABLE 6. MEAN SPECIFIC GRAVITY AND STANDARD DEVIATION FOR RIM- AND CORE-FACIES GRANODIORITE, ROCKY HILL STOCK, AND ULTRAMAFIC ROCKS, AMPHIBOLITE AND METAGABBRO FROM THE SURROUNDING COUNTRY ROCKS

| | Rocky Hill Granodiorite | | | Country Rocks | |
	Rim-Facies	Core-Facies	Ultramafic Rocks	Amphibolite	Metagabbro
Mean Specific Gravity ($\bar{x}$)	2.676	2.672	2.82	$3.08 \pm .01$	$2.93 \pm .01$
Standard Deviation(s)	0.003	0.008	0.18		
Number of Samples	19	18	16	2	2

mineral contents of rim- and core-facies rocks tend to be mutually compensating in their influence upon the specific gravity of the respective bulk rock samples. The mean values of the two facies are so close that no meaningful regional pattern in specific gravities which reflects the distribution of these rock types is to be expected. The values for metagabbro and amphibolite are from samples relatively near the contacts of the stock. The mean specific gravity of ultramafic rock samples taken near the stock is somewhat higher (2.895) than that for all samples included in Table 6, but the range of specific gravities obtained from ultramafic rocks up to 1.5 miles from the stock completely overlaps that of the former group.

Petrology and Petrogenesis of the Stock

INFERRED CRYSTALLIZATION HISTORY

A prime objective of this study is to reconstruct the crystallization history of the stock from the accumulated field and laboratory data. A satisfactory petrogenetic model for Rocky Hill must explain the spatial relationship of the two textural facies of granodiorite, the various features of the rock fabric and their distributions, and the patterns of regional variation in chemistry and modal mineralogy. Possible mechanisms or processes which could be invoked to explain the various features at Rocky Hill would include: (1) multiple intrusions of magma; (2) intrusion of a single inhomogeneous magma; (3) intrusion of a single magma which generally crystallizes from the walls inward or vice versa; (4) intrusion and crystallization of a single magma, with a progressive accumulation of volatiles in the residual liquid; (5) intrusion of a magma which reacts significantly with the wall rocks; and (6) emplacement of the pluton by some process of "granitization" not involving an intrusion of magma.

We believe that a model consistent with the greatest proportion of the observational data and the inferences that can most reasonably be derived from them would incorporate: (1) intrusion of a single magma, (2) crystallization from the walls inward, and (3) progressive increase of volatiles and attendant increase of vapor pressure in the residual melt. The facts and inferences pertinent to this conclusion, and to the rejection of other models are discussed below. Basically, this supporting data shows or implies that: (1) liquid magma existed longer in the core area of the stock; (2) mineral phases in the core area crystallized in large part later than their counterparts in rocks nearer the margins; and (3) in the core area these same minerals crystallized for the most part under a higher prevailing pressure of dissolved volatiles.

Relationship of Rim- and Core-Facies Granodiorite and Aplites

The relative spatial positions of the two facies of granodiorite is a distinctive petrologic feature of the Rocky Hill stock. The gradational nature, both texturally and compositionally, of the boundary between the rim- and core-facies, the lack of inclusions or dikes of one rock in the other, and the lack of distinctive textures which might result from a mixing of magmas argue against a mechanism of separate intrusion for these rocks.

The matrix of the subporphyritic core-facies is mineralogically and compositionally similar to the aplites (Putman and Alfors, 1965, p. 360), and all large aplite dikes either issue from, transect, or are otherwise closely associated with rocks which have more than 10 percent matrix. Numerous small segregations of aplite-pegmatite are also present in the core-facies rocks. We interpret the fine-grained matrix of the core-facies granodiorite as representing the liquid portion of the magma which was present in the core area after most, if not all, of the rim-facies granodiorite had crystallized. The aplite dikes and segregations are believed to represent some of the residual melt of the core area which was either injected into fractures formed in the adjacent solid rock or remained as segregations in the core area when the melt became saturated in volatiles. The fine-grained texture of the matrix in the core-facies and related granodiorite is interpreted as a result of more or less isothermal quenching which was caused by loss of volatile pressure at the time of aplite injection (Putman and Alfors, 1965, p. 359). Younger aplite dikes crosscut and offset older aplites in several outcrops thus indicating that aplite injection occurred in several pulses. Similarly the matrix probably did not crystallize all at once, and the present distribution of matrix-bearing rocks and aplites is interpreted as indicating only where probable saturation of volatiles in the remaining liquid once occurred.

Pattern of Protoclastic Deformation

The reduced intensity of protoclastic deformation in the area of matrix-bearing rocks (Fig. 4) is another feature which we interpret as an indication that some liquid was present in these rocks until relatively late in the crystallization period. The residual liquid would serve to "cushion" the phenocrysts during intrusion and late magma movements in the stock.

Implications of Mineral Paragenesis and Modal Variations for a Residual Liquid

Petrographic observations previously noted indicate that the last primary minerals to crystallize in the rim-facies granodiorite were quartz, potassium feldspar, and sodic plagioclase of about An_{10}. These same minerals are the main phases (>97 percent) of the aplites and the matrix of the core-facies granodiorite—a further indication that these latter units are appropriate crystallization products of a residual liquid developed by the earlier partial crystallization of the Rocky Hill granodiorite magma.

Modal differences between the rock facies, which might indicate the extent of crystallization differentiation, are a slightly lower mean content of potassium feldspar in the core-facies granodiorite and a marked decrease in the average amount of hornblende. The first modal change is not a common feature of differentiation in granitic rocks and will be discussed later. The decrease in the amount of hornblende is the main factor in a net decrease in total ferromagnesian minerals in the core-facies rocks. Replacement of hornblende by biotite does not appear any more extensive in the core-facies rocks than in the rim-facies rocks; thus the decrease in hornblende reflects some shift in the path of crystallization of the core-facies magma relative to that of the rim-facies magma.

This situation could be the result: (1) of decreased activity of calcium in the magma or increased activity of plagioclase during crystallization of the core-facies rocks; (2) of decrease in the total activity of iron and magnesium in the magma; and (3) of increase in the activity of potassium or volatiles in the magma while the ferromagnesian minerals were crystallizing.

Factors 1 and 2 apply in some degree because in the core-facies rocks the average plagioclase content is higher though the calcium content is the same or slightly lower, and the mean total Fe + Mg content is slightly lower. The relative differences between rock facies are small, however, and it is difficult to say whether such small changes could produce the observed decrease in the amount of hornblende. The average biotite content in the core-facies rocks is nearly the same as that in the rim-facies despite slightly less Fe + Mg and K_2O. This suggests that, in the core-facies rocks, crystallization of biotite was favored, rather than hornblende, either because of a higher activity (pressure) of volatiles (H_2O + F primarily), or because a sufficiently high activity occurred *at an earlier stage of crystallization* of the magma.

Distribution of Deuteric Alteration

A visual record of the relative amounts of volatiles in different portions of the stock is provided by the pattern of deuteric alteration (Fig. 8). Only the intensity of chloritization of the ferromagnesian phases is plotted in Figure 8, but sericitization of sodic plagioclase and other changes in the rock are also involved, as previously noted. The distribution of deuteric chlorite is strikingly similar to the distributions of core-facies rocks (Fig. 2) and of rocks containing matrix (Fig. 5), and lends further support to the inference that these rocks represent the sites of volatile-saturated, residual liquid.

Fractionation Trends as Shown by Regional Changes in Phase Composition

One of the strongest lines of evidence bearing on the crystallization history of the Rocky Hill stock is provided by the patterns of regional trace element fractionation in the ferromagnesian phases. Fractionation on a small scale is evident in the zoning of some of the mineral grains of the granodiorite, but direct evidence of regional fractionation at Rocky Hill by means of areal changes in the amount, type, or composition (major constituents) of mineral phases is not provided by the sampling plan used in this study. However, in igneous rocks in general, relatively more variation occurs in trace element content among rock samples, or phases from them, than for major constituents, and such is the case at Rocky Hill (Putman and Alfors, 1967). Accordingly, as a more effective means of depicting regional fractionation during crystallization, considerable attention was devoted to determining whether significant areal variations in the content of trace elements occurred in the ferromagnesia phases.

In the previous section dealing with analytical results, the influence of the distribution of magnetite upon the trace element data obtained from the ferromagnesian phases was pointed out. It can be seen in Table 4 that magnetite at Rocky Hill generally contains important amounts of Cr, Cu, V, and Zn, and a notably lower content of Ni, relative to the ferromagnesian phase. In order to derive meaningful regional patterns of variation, it is necessary to adjust the Cr, Cu, Ni, V, and Zn analyses from each ferromagnesian separate for the amount of magnetite present in the rock sample; therefore, all samples were adjusted to a common reference of zero magnetite content. Further details of the calculation of the required adjustment are in Appendix II.

Regional variation in the adjusted trace element data was studied by trend-surface analysis. A number of accounts of the theory and application of trend surface analysis to geological data have been published. Those of Whitten (1959, 1961), Whitten and Boyer (1964), Dawson and Whitten (1962), Baird and others (1966), Baird and others (1967a), and Baird and others (1967b) are probably most pertinent to the application in this work, and no detailed discussion of the method will be made here. Relevant statistical data for the trend-surface components shown here and for surfaces of other degree are included in Table 7.

Trend surfaces of relatively high order, compared to most of the applications cited above, were used to describe the Rocky Hill data in the figures which follow. This approach is warranted for several reasons. (1) All fifth-degree trend-surface components have confidence levels greater than 95 percent, and half of the eighth degree surfaces exceed 99 percent confidence. (2) The contribution of background "noise" to the total variability has been estimated previously in Table 4. This contribution consists of analytical error plus local or within-grid variability, and will be included in the deviations observed from a particular trend surface. However, there is no evidence in this

TABLE 7. ANALYSIS OF VARIANCE FOR FERROMAGNESIAN PHASE
TRACE METAL DATA USED IN FIGURES 12-17

Variate	Sum of Squares (%)	Degrees of Freedom	Mean Square (%)	F Ratio	Confidence Level	Estimated Maximum Proportion (%) due to Regional Component of Variance
Due to						
Vanadium Surface 3rd Degree	15.4	9	1.71	2.85	>99)	
Deviations	84.6	141	0.60			
Vanadium Surface 5th Degree	21.3	20	1.07	1.76	>95)	65
Deviations	78.7	130	0.607			
Vanadium Surface 8th Degree	38.7	44	0.88	1.52	≅95)	—
Deviations	61.3	106	0.58			
Chromium Surface 3rd Degree	25.8	9	2.87	5.4	>>99)	
Deviations	74.2	140	0.53			
Chromium Surface 5th Degree	33.6	20	1.68	3.27	>99)	55.6
Deviations	66.4	129	0.515			
Chromium Surface 8th Degree	39.8	44	0.91	1.58	>95)	—
Deviations	60.2	105	0.575			
Nickel Surface 3rd Degree	37.6	9	4.18	9.44	>>99)	
Deviations	62.4	141	0.443			
Nickel Surface 5th Degree	47.8	20	2.39	5.96	>>99)	66
Deviations	52.2	130	0.402			
Nickel Surface 8th Degree	61.4	44	1.40	3.85	>>99)	—
Deviations	38.6	106	0.364			
Beryllium Surface 3rd Degree	56.6	9	6.29	20.4	>>99)	
Deviations	43.4	141	0.308			
Beryllium Surface 5th Degree	63.7	20	3.18	11.4	>>99)	69.8
Deviations	36.3	130	0.279			
Beryllium Surface 8th Degree	69.9	44	1.59	5.6	>>99)	—
Deviations	30.1	106	0.284			
Copper Surface 8th Degree	32.5	44	0.74	1.16	≅70)	48
Deviations	67.5	106	0.637			—
Zinc Surface 8th Degree	43.7	44	0.99	1.87	>99)	44.6
Deviations	56.3	106	0.53			—

*Rigorous application of trend surface analysis requires that normally distributed or normalized data be used, i.e. in the present case a logarithmic conversion of the trace metal data should be made (Putman and Alfors, 1967). However, the coefficients of variation of the original data are not large enough to introduce any significant error here if this conversion is neglected for the sake of convenience.

study that variability from this source is distributed in any systematic or non-random manner. (3) A complete orthogonal grid of data points is available for trace-element data on the exposed surface of the stock. The spacing of these points is close enough to provide adequate control for the additional detail which increasingly higher degree trend surface components are capable of providing. Apart from possible distortion along the margins of the grid, which is unimportant here, there is little risk of introducing spurious "patterns" which are not really present when a confidence level of 95 percent or more is indicated for the surface.

An estimate of the maximum possible proportion of real "trend" embodied in the total variance of each element is made in the last column of Table 7. This estimate is based upon a comparison of the relative variances obtained at the within-grid and within-pluton scales (Table 4) with no adjustment for analytical error, and it can be compared with the percent sums of squares associated with a particular trend surface (SSX_r). This situation would not necessarily exist in a sampling plan involving sample replication at every collecting site, whereby a direct estimate of the regional component of variance could be obtained (Baird and others, 1967a; Baird and others, 1967b).

Mandelbaum (1963) has used the mean square of the deviations from a trend surface (S.S. deviations/degrees freedom of deviations) as a criterion to judge the efficiency of the surface; the surface of the least deviation mean square then represents the best resolution of the regional from the random local variation. If this test is applied to the data of Table 7, then the fifth-degree surfaces for Cr and Be, and eighth-degree surfaces for V and Ni would appear to be optimum choices. To facilitate visual comparison, however, only the fifth-degree surfaces are shown in Figures 12 to 15.

The areal patterns of Cr, Ni, and V variation in the ferromagnesian phases (Figs. 12 to 14) are similar and indicate a very moderate but well-defined progressive fractionation trend in these elements toward the core of the stock. The behavior of these elements under conditions of fractional crystallization in magmatic systems is so well established as to require no comment here, and it provides strong evidence for progressive inward crystallization in the Rocky Hill stock. Figures 12 to 14 also exhibit similarity in the detail of the shape of the distribution patterns, which is evident in extensions of areas of lower value toward the northwest, southwest, and northeast (more weakly) margins of the stock. The northwest extension coincides with the northwest series of aplite dikes and zone of matrix-bearing rocks (Figs. 2 and 5), and is interpreted as indicating a relatively later crystallization of ferromagnesian phases in this portion of the stock (as well as in the other areas of lower

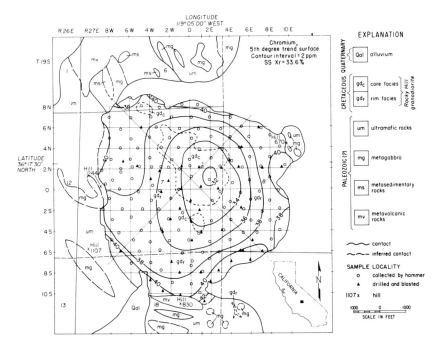

Figure 12. Chromium in ferromagnesian mineral phases, 5th degree trend surface. SSXr is the percent reduction in total sums of squares.

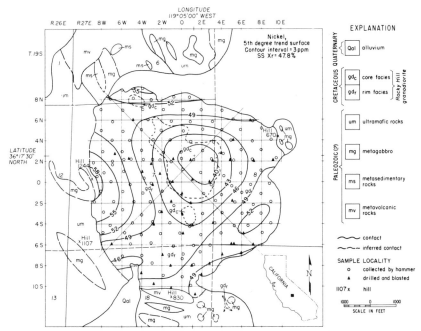

Figure 13. Nickel in ferromagnesian mineral phases, 5th degree trend surface.

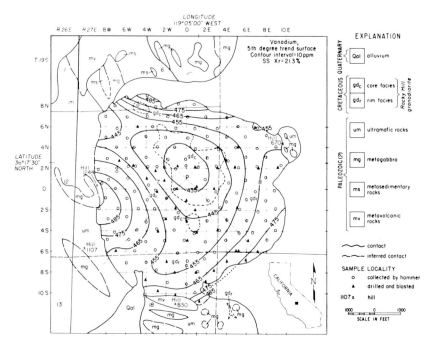

Figure 14. Vanadium in ferromagnesian mineral phases, 5th degree trend surface.

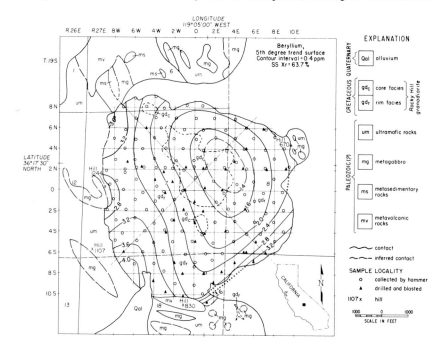

Figure 15. Beryllium in ferromagnesian mineral phases, 5th degree trend surface.

values). The pattern of closure on the isopleths, however, leaves little doubt that the last crystallizing ferromagnesian phases were in the core area. Since there appears to be a rather uniform paragenesis throughout the stock, the fractionation patterns for the ferromagnesian phases strongly imply a similar pattern for the relative sequence of crystallization of the rocks of the stock: that is, rocks of the core area were the last parts of the stock to crystallize. By sequence of crystallization it should be understood that we do not mean the paragenesis itself, but the *stage* of paragenesis attained at various points in the stock during crystallization of the magma.

The trend surface component for Be (Fig. 15) has a fractionation pattern similar to those of the ferro-metals. The change in Be content, however, is the reverse of its expected behavior during progressive magma differentiation. Unfortunately, data bearing on the magmatic behavior of Be is sparse and obviously more information is needed. A summary of much current analytical data can be found in Beus (1962).

Eighth-degree trend components for the distribution of Cu (Fig. 16) and Zn (Fig. 17) in the ferromagnesian phases were also prepared and will be discussed later in connection with the distribution of sulfide minerals. Neither

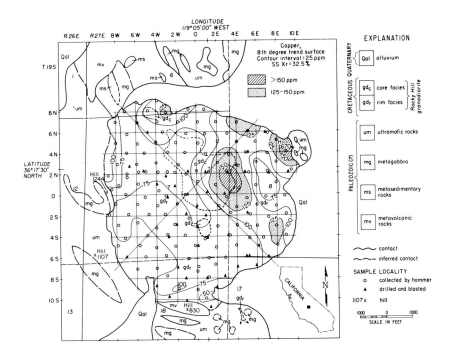

Figure 16. Copper in ferromagnesian mineral phases, 8th degree trend surface.

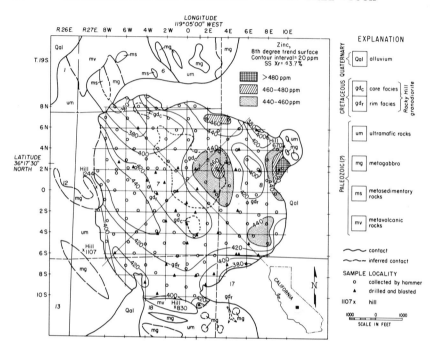

Figure 17. Zinc in ferromagnesian mineral phases, 8th degree trend surface.

of these elements shows any particular evidence of a direct response to the pattern of fractionation outlined heretofore, and apparently other factors are more important in influencing their distributions, although these factors themselves may be related to the crystallization sequence of the stock. The results of the trend surface analysis for Y are not included in this paper because of possible bias in the data. For example, the presence of 0.1 percent sphene in a ferromagnesian phase separate could change the Y content by 15 percent. Allanite might also be present, but would have a smaller effect. The trend components for Y do not indicate any meaningful patterns to the authors, but because of possible bias a significant trend may be obscured.

Other Indicators of Fractionation or Position of Residual Liquid

Rb_2O/K_2O ratios for biotite and potassium feldspar from a few samples of rim- and core-facies rocks are presented in Table 2. The ratios for both minerals appear significantly higher in core-facies rocks. Confidence in any inference based on this data must be tempered by the small number of samples involved, but the available data substantiate the fractionation pattern indicated by the trace elements discussed above.

A significant difference exists in the average fluorine content of biotite in the two rock facies (Table 2), and suggests that a relatively higher activity of fluorine was present during crystallization in the core-area of the stock. The available experimental data are limited to synthesis conditions for fluor-hydroxyl phlogopite (Noda and Ushio, 1964), and appear to indicate that a slight preference for OH^- exists in the mica relative to the H_2O/F ratio in the synthesis mixture at temperatures below 800°C. To the extent that this situation holds true for crystallization of biotite under magmatic conditions, fractional crystallization would tend to yield relatively higher fluorine contents in later crystals[3] and tend to increase the proportion of fluorine in the volatile fraction remaining in the magma.

Rarity of inclusions in the core-facies rock and the small size of those observed (none more than 3 inches) might be cited as one other possible indication of the persistence of residual liquid in this part of the stock. A relatively longer time interval during which liquid magma was present to react with inclusions, combined with the greater fluidity induced by a higher concentration of dissolved volatiles, would appear to be conditions tending to eliminate those inclusions that were present.

Implications of Fractionation and Assumptions

The existence of progressive regional fractionation and general inward crystallization of magma in the Rocky Hill stock appears to be confirmed by a wealth of supporting data. Fractionation on a regional scale in a plutonic body naturally implies that crystallization did not proceed simultaneously throughout the body, and that some transfer of residual material from the earlier to the later crystallizing portions of the body has taken place. The mechanism of such a transfer at Rocky Hill is not clear from the data collected. Apparently a slight amount of liquid was progressively shifted toward the core while an equivalent volume of crystals formed in the rim-facies or in a boundary zone such as that which now exists between the rock facies. If transfer by whatever mechanism does not occur, then the bulk chemistry of a rock sample, or phase from it, can only reflect primary compositional differences existing at the time of emplacement of magma (neglecting later alteration), and this condition will not be altered by the sequence of crystallization. Lack of a fractionation pattern, however, does not necessarily mean that simultaneous crystallization occurred, but only that transfer of material during crystallization was unlikely.

We do not believe that the fractionation trends for Rocky Hill are a result of primary compositional variation in the magma. Even if regional

---

[3]Provided that changes in $P_{volatiles}$ do not alter the substitution preference.

compositional variation in one or more elements existed in the Rocky Hill magma at the time of initial emplacement, there is no reason that such variation should result in similar patterns among several elements—all consistent with the same trend of regional fractionation—unless these elements had participated in a common magmatic crystallization sequence. Assimilation or reaction with wall rocks during emplacement of the stock also is incapable by itself of producing the observed fractionation trends, much for the same reason. Other factors arguing against contamination at Rocky Hill are: (1) lack of similarity in composition between inclusions and exposed wall rocks, and (2) lack of regional variation in major chemical constituents of a magnitude comparable to that for minor elements.

Perhaps a more serious aspect of the process of attempting to depict or estimate a regional variation pattern is the influence of possible variation in the vertical dimension. The maximum topographic relief at Rocky Hill is less than one sixth of the diameter of the stock and is not distributed in a manner which is suited to the study of vertical variation; indeed, one of the criteria in the selection of this pluton was the lack of rugged topography upon the surface to be sampled. The two-dimensional projections of the variability data shown here do not show any obvious relationship to the existing topography of the stock.

The problem of vertical components of variability in plutonic bodies has been discussed by Peikert (1962, 1965), who extended the conventional trend-surface-analysis method to provide a model for use in estimating three-dimensional specific gravity and mineralogical variation in the Glen Alpine stock. This model was also applied by Whitten and Boyer (1964) to modal data from the San Isabel granite. Although the importance of considering three-dimensional variation in plutonic bodies has been most properly emphasized by these authors, we do not consider the application of this model appropriate for the Rocky Hill data, nor for most variability data obtained by sampling a topographic surface. For such observations this model possesses an inherent bias in that it generates polynomial surfaces which tend to be subparallel to the topographic surface, or subdued replicas of it. Unless considerable local relief is present, the polynomial surfaces which are generated are not unique solutions. Peikert (1965) recognizes this problem, but from our standpoint does not adequately resolve it.

The scale of vertical variation in plutonic bodies still is a subject of some uncertainty. Visually obvious layering or gravitational accumulation of minerals is relatively unimportant in granitic plutons, and, where structural and fabric elements of the rock body indicate a sense of subvertical rather than subhorizontal displacement, it appears unrealistic to us to think of vertical mineralogical or chemical gradients which are appreciably greater than those occurring in two dimensions. For the present we can only conclude that little evidence exists at Rocky Hill to suggest that the fractionation trends previously shown are subject to significant change at least within a vertical range of 1000 feet. This does not imply, however, that vertical variation in chemical composition is absent in the Rocky Hill stock or that relative vertical movements of the residual magma during crystallization did not take place.

Crystallization of Magma and Mineral Paragenesis

A tacit assumption throughout this discussion is that the Rocky Hill granodiorite is a product of magmatic crystallization. This assumption is substantiated by many of the observations cited previously for all scales of the investigation. An instructive aspect of this crystallization is to compare the paragenesis of major mineral phases, as inferred from petrographic observation, with crystallization trends predicted by consideration of the system $NaAlSi_3O_8$-$CaAl_2Si_2O_8$-$KAlSi_3O_8$-SiO_2-H_2O (hereafter these components are abbreviated as Ab-An-Or-Q-H_2O). Phase equilibria of this system are considered to be a reasonable approximation for the course of crystallization of the major phases of the granodiorite since the normative total of Ab, An, Or, and Q is about 90 percent. Current experimental work has been concerned with the quaternary boundary portions of this system so that quantitative relationships are not yet available for the behavior of compositions inside. Qualitative description of the paths of crystallization and the general nature of the phase fields is possible, however, and provides a frame of reference for considering the paragenesis data of the Rocky Hill stock.

Figure 18 is a diagrammatic representation of phase relations in the condensed system Ab-An-Or-Q as an isobaric tetrahedral projection. The P_{H_2O} for such a projection is sufficient to cause the four-phase boundary curve (orthoclase-quartz-plagioclase-liquid) to intersect or to closely approach the Ab-Or-Q face. In Figure 18, the bulk composition of the granodiorite is represented by the point x. If this composition were entirely liquid, crystallization of a small amount of plagioclase would drive the liquid composition to the quartz-plagioclase boundary surface, whereupon quartz would also crystallize. This condition appears to correspond to the initial state of the granodiorite magma, with the liquid containing phenocrysts of plagioclase (about An_{45}), and possibly quartz, and lying very near or on the quartz-plagioclase boundary surface. Both quartz and zoned plagioclase appear to have a long paragenesis at Rocky Hill, which should be the case if these phases began crystallizing early (or were already present as phenocrysts in the initial magma). The presence of zoning in mineral grains is evidence that fractional crystallization occurred, therefore only the outer portions of growing crystals can be considered to be in equilibrium with the magma at any given stage of crystallization.

With further isobaric crystallization of quartz and plagioclase, the composition of the remaining liquid would move in a curved path along the quartz-plagioclase surface toward the boundary of the potassium feldspar field (Fig. 18). Concurrently, the plagioclase crystals would become progressively

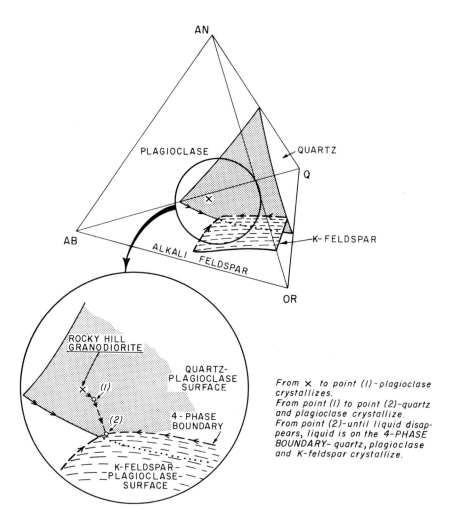

Figure 18. Isobaric tetrahedral projection of field boundaries at the liquidus in the system Or($KAlSi_3O_8$) - Ab($NaAlSi_3O_8$) - AN($CaAl_2Si_2O_8$) - Q(SiO_2) - H_2O. This representation is diagrammatic only and is not intended to be quantitatively accurate. Or-Ab-An face from data of Yoder and others (1957). An-Q join from data of Stewart (1958). Q-Or-Ab face from data of Tuttle and Bowen (1958).

more sodic in the outer zones. When the composition of the liquid reached the four-phase boundary line, potassium feldspar would crystallize along with quartz and plagioclase. This latter situation appears to have occurred in the Rocky Hill granodiorite when roughly 50 to 60 percent of the rock had crystallized, as inferred from the proportion of matrix in some core-facies rocks, and it agrees well with the late paragenesis of potassium feldspar. Judging from the aplite compositions (Putman and Alfors, 1965), the anorthite content of the remaining liquid at the advent of potassium feldspar crystallization is An_3 or less, and the liquid composition has approached the Ab-Or-Q face of Figure 18. Experimental work by Tuttle and Bowen (1958) suggested that the four-phase boundary would actually intersect the "ternary" (Ab-Or-Q) phase boundary[4] to produce a quaternary eutectic, with two alkali feldspars co-existing with liquid and quartz, only at pressures exceeding 3.4 kilobars P_{H_2O}. At lower pressures only a single alkali feldspar would be in equilibrium with a liquid of very low anorthite content, and the four-phase boundary line would be terminated within the tetrahedron.

There is no textural evidence of a single alkali feldspar having existed late in the paragenesis at Rocky Hill, and the zoned perthitic potassium feldspar which is present does not appear to have once had an over-all bulk composition more sodic than $Or_{70}Ab_{30}$. It is possible that some of the aplites at Rocky Hill have recrystallized from an initial hypersolvus condition, or even from a glass, but the granodiorite appears to have completed crystallization essentially as a subsolvus, two-feldspar rock. The P_{H_2O} during crystallization of the Rocky Hill granodiorite, however, does not appear to have exceeded 2 kb, as inferred from evidence discussed below. Some additional lowering of liquidus temperatures because of the presence of fluorine would reduce the P_{H_2O} required to produce a quaternary eutectic, but even with this effect the petrographic data would be better explained in terms of a wider feldspar solvus. The small CaO content of the last crystallizing liquid is thus a significant factor in increasing solvus temperatures, possibly also aided by the effect of the relative thermal state of the potassium feldspar phase. The mineralogy and normative calculations for the whole rock do not suggest that a molar excess of $Na_2O + K_2O$ was present during feldspar crystallization to thus promote the latter effect (Luth and Tuttle, 1966), but the time factor in comparing results of relatively short-term experimental runs on the alkali-feldspar solvus to plutonic crystallization cannot be adequately evaluated.

---

[4]That is, the liquidus minimum in the Q-Or-Ab "ternary" system intersects the alkali feldspar solvus.

Summary and Reconstruction of Crystallization History

We feel that the accumulated field and laboratory evidence cited here provides a consistent and substantial basis for the construction of a petrologic model for Rocky Hill. The general picture emerges quite clearly, even though of necessity some details must be tentative. We conclude that the Rocky Hill stock was emplaced as a primarily vertical intrusion of granodiorite magma which progressively crystallized from the walls inward. Rise of the remaining magma in the intrusion continued while crystallization proceeded and the bulk of the rim-facies granodiorite formed. The last part of the rim-facies granodiorite to solidify was near the northwest contact of the stock. This may represent the path of late magma additions, or the area of latest expansion of the initial intrusion. At this point in the crystallization sequence, approximately 75 percent of the stock (at the present level of exposure), consisted of solid or nearly solid granodiorite. Crystallization of this portion of the granodiorite progressively increased the amount of volatiles dissolved in the residual magma, and some portions of this magma became saturated, particularly the portion near the northwest contact. Saturation is considered here to have developed when vapor pressure of the melt equaled the confining pressure of the rock load above (Putman and Alfors, 1965). Saturation resulted in rupture of the adjacent solid rock and intrusion of some of the liquid portion of the residual magma to form aplite dikes. A consequent loss of the vapor pressure by this mechanism then caused an essentially isothermal "quench" of magma to produce a rock with a fine-grained matrix. Following solidification or isolation of the matrix-bearing rocks on the northwest margin of the stock, recurrent saturation, rupture and intrusion, and quenching continued in the residual magma to produce the bulk of the core-facies granodiorite.

INTERPRETATION OF PETROGRAPHIC AND MODAL FEATURES AND THEIR DISTRIBUTIONS

Some observations cited previously do not in themselves provide any direct implications concerning the crystallization history of the stock. However, the intrusion model outlined above constitutes a petrologic framework into which other facts and inferences may be fitted. In this section, some of the possible relationships of these observations will be discussed.

Modal Variation of Feldspars and Zoning of Plagioclase

Real differences in modal plagioclase and potassium feldspar appear to exist between the rim- and core-facies granodiorite; the core-facies has a slightly lower content of potassium feldspar and a higher content of plagioclase (Fig. 10). This situation is in part the opposite of modal variation in many granitic plutons cited in the literature, where the core or central rock units tend to contain higher modal quartz and potassium feldspar, and a lower color index.[5] We do not, however, regard the Rocky Hill modal distributions as unique, but only as a variation induced by the conditions of the crystallization sequence. If, as appears highly probable, inward crystallization of the Rocky Hill granodiorite stock was accompanied by a progressive increase in P_{H_2O} until the residual liquid was saturated, then the change in the composition of the liquidus minima in the "granite" system with increasing P_{H_2O} provides a possible explanation for the observed modal variation. A residual liquid derived as a result of crystallization of the rim-facies granodiorite at a P_{H_2O} of less than 1 kb would contain about 28 weight percent Or molecule (Fig. 19). At a P_{H_2O} of 1.5 to 2 kb, a residual liquid such as that which accumulated in the core-facies granodiorite would contain about 25 weight percent Or, or the same amount as that found in the analysed aplites (Putman and Alfors, 1965). If the proportion of liquid in the magma of the core-facies granodiorite at the onset of potassium feldspar crystallization is roughly 50 percent,[6] (that is, 50 percent of the magma has crystallized as quartz, plagioclase, and biotite plus accessories), this would result in a rock with 12.5 weight percent potassium feldspar—an amount equivalent to the average mode of the core-facies granodiorite.

Injection of aplite dikes and segregation of aplitic material would also account for a net removal of potassium feldspar from the core-facies granodiorite, and they are undoubtedly minor contributing factors to the observed modal differences. "Filter pressing," or transfer of residual liquid within the crystal mesh of partially crystallized magma, may be indicated by the relatively large modal variations in potassium feldspar and plagioclase which occur between slab sections of a single hand specimen of some transitional core-facies rocks (2S-3E, for example). Some outcrops of this rock type have a patchy or inhomogeneous distribution of textures and grain size (3N-4E, 0-3E).

Plagioclase from most of the rim-facies granodiorite exhibits progressive normal zoning with some abrupt compositional changes and some delicate fine oscillations within the zones. The embayed condition of some of the plagioclase cores may be the result of rise of the magma during intrusion, with a decrease in load pressure lowering the melting point; the abrupt compositional changes between zones may represent changes in P_{H_2O} during

---

[5]Examples include: Dawson and Whitten, 1962; Peikert, 1965; Taubeneck, 1957, 1964; Davis, 1963; and Compton, 1955.

[6]Approximately the amount of matrix observed in core-facies rocks in which potassium feldspar is essentially confined to the matrix.

crystallization, or, for those in interior portions of crystals, perhaps differential flow or cycling of the magma. Some influence of diffusion in the magmatic liquid during crystal growth seems indicated by the fine oscillations of some zones, but the erratic style of plagioclase zoning, even within a single thin section, does not lend itself to general inferences about the crystallization history of the stock. In the interior of the stock, plagioclase grains consistently have a single relatively broad reverse zone near their margins as shown in Figure 5. It would seem that this zoning distribution is a function of the crystallization sequence already outlined, but at present a specific cause is not obvious. The crystallization of plagioclase with a composition of about An_{20} might be prolonged late in the crystallization history because of three possibilities. (1) An increase in the composition gap between the plagioclase solidus and the residual liquid might occur under a condition of progressively

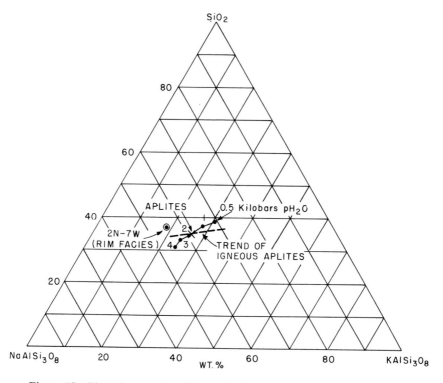

Figure 19. Plot of normative albite, orthoclase, and quartz (recalculated to 100 per cent) for the Rocky Hill samples. Progressive shift of the quaternary isobaric minima or eutectic in the system $NaAlSi_3O_8$ - $KAlSi_3O_8$ - SiO_2 - H_2O with increasing P_{H_2O} is also shown (compositions are projected to the anhydrous base of the tetrahedron).

increasing P_{H_2O} In other words, sodic plagioclase of a given composition would continue to crystallize while P_{H_2O} increased and the anorthite content of the remaining liquid decreased within small limits. (2) An accumulation and transfer of residual liquid toward the core area of the stock would tend to increase the potential amount of sodic plagioclase in the rocks of this area. (3) A differential flow or convection of the magma in the core area would cause physical transfer of plagioclase crystals both laterally and vertically.

Slight reverse zoning near the margins of sodic plagioclase might then be a result of the rate at which P_{H_2O} increased (or was lost when the residual magma became saturated), relative to movements of either plagioclase crystals or portions of the residual liquid.

Distribution of Magnetite

The distribution of magnetite in bulk rock samples is shown in Figure 6. Variation in magnetite content on the local or outcrop scale tends to be relatively small (determined by susceptibility measurements on duplicate samples and magnetometer traverses on outcrop areas of granodiorite), and it is not considered to be a significant factor in the plot of Figure 6. Although the ferromagnesian mineral assemblage and amount of magnetite in a given rock sample reflect the nature of oxidation-reduction equilibria prevailing during magmatic crystallization, it is difficult to interpret Figure 6 in terms of any control or influence exerted by the crystallization sequence of the stock.

In granitic magmas, a natural partial buffering of oxygen fugacity[7] is provided by ferrous-ferric iron in the melt and in crystalline phases. Ordinarily, oxygen fugacities indicated by the phase assemblages of granitic rocks are several orders of magnitude lower than would be the case if oxygen fugacity was controlled by the dissociation of water dissolved in the magma (Loomis, 1964); consequently, correspondingly higher hydrogen fugacities (example: fH_2 approaches 1 bar in a system at 2 kb P_{H_2O} and $800°C$ with fO_2 of the Ni-NiO buffer, Eugster and Wones, 1962) are apparently present. Relative diffusion of hydrogen from the magma would then be a potential factor in promoting oxidation of iron in the magma or in inducing higher oxygen fugacities during crystallization. In a plutonic magma body, loss of hydrogen to the walls could promote the crystallization of magnetite at the expense of iron-bearing silicate mineral phases in the border zones or contacts of the pluton. Much of the granodiorite with the highest magnetite content at Rocky Hill is near the margins of the stock, but not exclusively so, and areas where magnetite is absent or very low also do not have a unique location within the

---

[7]The term oxygen fugacity (fO_2) is used here in the same sense as noted by Fudali (1965), and it does not imply the existence of a discrete gas phase in the magma.

stock. Whether a mechanism of hydrogen diffusion can be invoked to explain these distributions is at this point a matter of speculation.

Sample O-3E is from the southern portion of an area of core- and transitional-facies granodiorite which is characterized by an accumulation of sulfide minerals in accessory amounts. This sample itself contains no magnetite, and both the bulk rock and biotite from it are notable for relatively low ferric iron contents (Table 2). In this particular sample, the late introduction of sulfides appears to have resulted in reduction of much of the ferric iron and replacement of any magnetite once present by pyrrhotite and chalcopyrite. Kullerud and Yoder (1964) studied iron-bearing silicate-sulfur reactions experimentally, and suggested that an introduction of sulfur into a silicate system results in the oxidation of some iron in silicates (to produce oxidized forms of the minerals or iron oxide phases) as well as the formation of an iron sulfide phase. The recognition of such oxidation in the mineral assemblage of a rock body was also suggested as a possible guide for use in exploration for sulfide mineralization. This use of oxidation, however, would appear to be limited to conditions of low P_{H_2O} or "dry" systems as in the experimental runs. Under hydrothermal conditions where H_2O is present in addition to sulfur, the relative oxidation or reduction of iron in silicate minerals is in general dependent upon equilibria among H_2, O_2, H_2S, and SO_2 as well.

Distribution of Sulfides and the Distribution of Copper and Zinc in Ferromagnesian Phases

The distribution of sulfides in the Rocky Hill stock is shown in Figure 7. Sulfide concentrations are contoured on an approximately logarithmic interval, for the highest concentrations observed are 100 times or more those of the lowest. Pyrite, chalcopyrite, and pyrrhotite are the main sulfide phases in order of probable abundance, but are not differentiated in Figure 7 because of difficulty in identifying these phases on weathered outcrops. The area of highest sulfide concentration is well defined and localized in an area of core-facies and transitional rocks between 1E and 4E. Sulfides (mainly pyrite) are also observed in aplite dikes adjacent to and within the core-facies area, and in some aplites of the northwest-trending series near 7N-8W. The most conspicuous concentration of sulfides in aplite, however, occurs in the large dike which trends southeast from locality 0-2E and contains pyrite, chalcopyrite, and molybdenite.

Eighth-degree trend-surface plots for the distribution of Cu and Zn in ferromagnesian phases are shown in Figures 16 and 17. The level of confidence for the Zn plot exceeds 98 percent (*see* Table 7), while that for Cu is approximately 70 percent. An eighth-degree trend-surface representation is used here for both elements in order to provide more detail. A regional fractionation trend similar to those displayed by other trace elements (Figs. 12 to 15) does not appear to be present for Cu or Zn. The area of highest copper content in the ferromagnesian phase coincides with that of the maximum sulfide content, however this coincidence is primarily due to chalcopyrite inclusions in the ferromagnesian phase. The maximum copper content actually in solid solution in the ferromagnesian phase is estimated to be 200 to 250 ppm from considerations of the frequency distribution of copper (Putman and Alfors, 1967) and from HF decomposition tests on a ferromagnesian phase separate from sample 4N-7E. Preliminary analyses of the separate from sample 0-3E within the sulfide zone indicate a maximum copper content of less than 25 ppm actually in solid solution. In the case of Zn, the authors profess some uncertainty as to the adequacy of the magnetite compensation made for the raw ferromagnesian phase data. A strong compensation factor produces a general fractionation pattern similar to Figures 12-15, but with Zn increasing toward the core of the stock. The local highs of Figure 17 are then retained as local features on the general pattern. Regardless of whether this interpretation should be made, the areas of highest zinc content in the ferromagnesian phase are not closely related to the sulfide distribution, and sulfide inclusions would have little effect, for no major zinc-bearing sulfide phases are present.[8] The distributions of Figures 7, 16, and 17 suggest that during crystallization of the rim-facies granodiorite concentrations of copper and zinc in the magma were locally higher on the east side of the stock. Crystallization of the interior of the stock and subsequent deuteric alteration proceeded under a relatively higher activity of volatiles, including sulfur, and resulted in a local concentration of sulfide phases in the core-facies and neighboring transitional granodiorite. The transfer and accumulation of chalcophile elements under the influence of higher sulfur (and possibly fluorine) concentrations late in the paragenesis of the granodiorite may have involved leaching of these elements from the existing ferromagnesian silicate and metallic oxide phases of the surrounding granodiorite. However, the data of Figures 7, 16, and 17 as well as the preliminary analytical data cited above do not exclude a process whereby chalcophile elements tend to be retained in the magma under the same conditions.

Variability in zinc content of the ferromagnesian phase is relatively low on both the regional and local scales (Table 4), whereas that for copper is one of the highest observed in this study. In spite of this contrast in behavior, the distribution patterns of Figures 16 and 17 are remarkably similar in the

---

[8]Whether such phases might have existed above this level of exposure cannot be answered.

arrangement of highs and lows; a fact which we interpret as indicating that Cu and Zn responded similarly during most of the crystallization sequence of silicate minerals in the granodiorite.

The maximum sulfide concentration at Rocky Hill equals the grade of hypogene zone of many copper-molybdenum ore bodies of the "porphyry" type, but the sulfide zone is too small in area to assume any economic importance. The situation is one of scale only, however, and the existence of the sulfide zone provides some indication as to the efficiency of rock and mineral sampling as a prospecting guide. In earlier work, a tentative suggestion was made that analysis of the mafic mineral phases of granitic rocks might serve as an indication of anomalous metal contents (Putman and Burnham, 1963). In the light of our experience at Rocky Hill, the latter suggestion is subject to severe limitation as a guide to common sulfide ores of igneous affinity. In particular, variability of the copper content of the ferromagnesian and metallic oxide phases of granitic rocks tends to be relatively high, and relatively steep gradients in the copper content of these phases appear to exist on a very local scale (Fig. 16; Putman and Alfors, 1967). In addition, the presence of accessory chalcopyrite in the rock may not be reflected in an above-average copper content of any of the associated silicate or oxide mineral phases. Thus, at Rocky Hill, sulfide mineralization is not revealed or suggested by the distribution of copper and zinc values in silicate phases in most of the granodiorite outside of the main sulfide-bearing zone. Obviously, analysis of bulk rock samples or their heavy fractions provides a better basis for estimating metal contents or for determining metal dispersion patterns related to mineralization.

ESTIMATION OF PHYSICAL CONDITIONS DURING EMPLACEMENT AND CRYSTALLIZATION

Knowledge of the physical conditions attending the genesis of plutonic rock bodies is an elusive goal sought by petrologists. Proper interpretation of field and laboratory data, and the reconstruction of former processes are often only possible through the information gained from experimental work on synthetic systems. Unfortunately, direct comparison or extrapolation of

---

[9]Sample 2N-7W, for example, yields a few ppm copper in weak-acid extraction tests and very small amounts of sulfides can be observed in the outcrop. Similar extraction tests on the biotite from 2N-7W were negative and spectrochemical analysis indicated a Cu content of 70 ppm in the biotite, an amount below the mean Cu content of all ferromagnesian samples. A similar situation exists in sulfide-rich sample 0-3E as previously stated.

experimental data (including work on the rocks themselves) to natural plutonic rocks is usually subject to some degree of limitation since nature: (1) provides plenty of chemical components; (2) probably always provides for dynamic change in physical conditions during formation of the rock or pluton; (3) provides a relative immensity of time and scale in which to carry out a variety of processes; and (4) leaves the final product in various states of alteration and exposure with some components missing, depleted, transferred, or enhanced.

Nevertheless, estimation of physical conditions from experimental data can be quite precise for some stages or some products of petrogenesis, and in other cases a sufficiently close approximation can be made such that a diagnostic interpretation is possible. In still other cases where an apparent conflict arises between the interpretation of the field data and the relevant experimental results, a means of solution through further observation from either source may be suggested.

In this section, we shall attempt to estimate some of the physical conditions which prevailed during some stages of the crystallization history of the Rocky Hill stock, and discuss various qualifications involved in the derivation of these estimates.

P_{H_2O} and the Depth of Intrusion

In a previous paper (Putman and Alfors, 1965, P_{H_2O} of the volatile-saturated magma was estimated by comparison of the composition of aplites with the position of the quaternary isobaric liquidus minimum in the system $Ab-Or-Q-H_2O$. This comparison is still considered valid, at least in theory, but the earlier aplite data should be corrected for a slight compositional bias due to the presence of scattered phenocrysts of quartz and zoned plagioclase. The revised average normative aplite composition, recalculated to 100 percent $Ab+Or+Q$, is then Or - 26.5 percent, Ab - 38 percent, and Q - 35.5 percent. Comparison with the positions of projected isobaric quaternary minima in the system $Ab-Or-Q-H_2O$ (Fig. 19; Jahns and Tuttle, 1963) indicates that a pressure of 1.5 to 2 kb existed when the aplites were emplaced.

The accuracy of this estimate is subject to several qualifications whose effects are as yet unknown. A plot of normative Ab, Or, and Q for representative igneous aplites shown by Tuttle and Jahns (1968) forms a nearly straight line near the trend of minima in the "granite" system, and intersects it at a point corresponding to about 2 kb P_{H_2O} (Fig. 19). The Rocky Hill aplites, then, are not diagnostic in composition and could fall on either trend. The difference in the two plots for other normative compositions, however, does pose a problem for the use of aplite compositions in general for estimating P_{H_2O}. Shift of the trend of isobaric quaternary minima could be a result: (1) of the presence of other volatiles in addition to H_2O, and (2) of the presence of solid phases of lower thermal state in equilibrium at the liquidus, that is, the stable potassium-feldspar phase at the liquidus may be a sanidine of lower temperature structural state than those which are present in relatively short-term experimental runs on synthetic materials (O. F. Tuttle, 1966, oral commun.). Fluorine is known to have been present in the volatile fraction during formation of the core-facies granodiorite at Rocky Hill, but the relative effect of this on the composition of the liquidus minimum is at present unknown.[10]

A previous estimate of the depth of intrusion of the stock (Putman and Alfors, 1965) was based on the assumption of equivalence of P_{H_2O} and static load pressure on saturated magma. Although protoclastic deformation effects in the granodiorite are not absent, as was implied earlier, there is no evidence that external tectonic stresses played any part in controlling the intrusion of aplites or in providing fractures for escape of volatiles. Except for the thin shear zones and local areas of crude foliation at the margins of the stock or in the rim-facies granodiorite, a planar orientation of protoclastic deformation features is absent in the rock fabric. Although the orientation of the aplite dike series in the northwest quadrant of the stock approximates that of the planar grain fracture and a major joint set as represented on Figures 2 and 3, these latter elements are younger than the aplites and in outcrop are observed to cut across them.

The existence of numerous small aplite segregations with occasional inner pegmatites in the core-facies granodiorite, which are not visibly related to any dike, would appear to be further evidence that saturation of the magma resulted from an internal pressure of volatiles which equalled or slightly exceeded the confining pressure. Using an average density of 2.8 gm/cc as assumed previously, the estimated depth of intrusion is then 5.5 to 7 km. The accuracy of this estimate is, of course, directly (but not solely) dependent upon the estimate of $P_{volatiles}$. Bateman and Wahrhaftig (1966, p. 125) allude to recent information which casts doubt on the validity of the assumption that $P_{H_2O} = P_{load}$, and certainly this is not a valid general assumption during plutonic crystallization, nor is the mere existence of aplites a sufficient basis for this assumption. However, the inferences upon which P_{H_2O} was equated with

---

[10]The experimental work of Wyllie and Tuttle (1961) on the effects of HF and H_2O upon the melting of "granite" suggests that the depression of liquidus temperatures by HF may be accompanied by expansion of the quartz field (projected into the system Ab, Or, Q) at the expense of feldspar. Because of migration of material in the vapor phase during the experiments, however, the magnitude of this effect is unknown and no extrapolation to natural magmas is possible. Shift of the ternary isobaric minimum in the Ab. Or, Q system reflects expansion of the quartz field with increasing P_{H_2O}, and if HF has a similar effect, the assumption of P volatiles = P_{H_2O} used here will lead to overestimation of vapor pressures.

P_{load} for the Rocky Hill stock (Putman and Alfors, 1965) are drawn from a particular case and are thought to be valid.

With the available data, an estimate of P_{H_2O} or water content of the magma at the time of intrusion is little more than pure speculation. Further discussion on this point is deferred to the section where an estimate of biotite stability conditions is made.

Temperature During Intrusion and Magmatic Crystallization

A temperature corresponding to the close of magmatic crystallization and the intrusion of aplites can be estimated by comparison with the temperatures of liquidus minima in the Ab, Or, Q, H_2O system. At a P_{H_2O} of 2 kb, the "granite" minimum lies at about 690°C (Tuttle and Bowen, 1958), and this temperature can be cited as a probable upper limit for for Rocky Hill. Results from a limited number of experimental runs (Appendix Table 2) made on water-saturated Rocky Hill aplite establish that at 1 kb the solidus is between 700°C and 750°C and at 2 kb the solidus is below 700°C, which is in excellent agreement with previous experimental work in the granite system. Extrapolation from these results to provide more exact estimates of the conditions in the Rocky Hill magma is limited, however, by the possible effects of volatiles other than water and the longer time interval over which equilibrium was established, or approached. Marked depression of liquidus temperatures occurs with small amounts of fluorine (Wyllie and Tuttle, 1961), and with 5 weight percent HF in the volatile fraction the "granite" liquidus lies near 650°C. Considering the proportion of fluorine in the biotite of corefacies granodiorite and the synthesis data for fluor-hydroxyl-phlogopite (Noda and Ushio, 1964), the presence of at least 5 weight percent HF in the volatile fraction[11] appears very reasonable. Larger amounts of HF do not produce much additional depression of the liquidus, thus a temperature of 650°C is estimated for the last stages of magmatic crystallization at Rocky Hill. The possible effect of fluorine in shifting the composition of liquids at the minimum in the "granite" system has been noted previously, and to this extent the estimates of both temperature and $P_{volatiles}$ may require revision.

An estimate of temperature at the time of intrusion or of the first stages of the crystallization sequence is more difficult, and, in reality, a range of temperatures is probably involved. A temperature at which crystals in the liquid consist only of relict cores of plagioclase grains with a composition of approximately An_{42}, and possibly quartz, is thought to simulate the conditions in the

---

[11]Small amounts of P_2O_5, CO_2, and H_2S are also believed to have been present, but are not considered to have a significant effect here.

magma at the time of intrusion to those crustal levels now exposed. Current experimental data are not complete enough to enable a precise estimation of temperature for a magma of Rocky Hill composition and condition, and any estimate is dependent upon the value of P_{H_2O} assumed or estimated for the initial intrusion. Results from a limited number of hydrothermal runs (Appendix Table 2) made on Rocky Hill granodiorite indicate that at 1 kb the liquidus is between 800°C and 850°C. The initial crystallization product was plagioclase with a composition of $An_{40 \pm 5}$. This composition was determined by X-ray diffractometry using the angular separation $(2\theta(1\bar{1}1) - 2\theta(\bar{2}01))$ and the curve for synthetic plagioclase given by Smith and Gay (1958, Fig. 2, p. 754). Quartz apparently began crystallizing between 750°C and 800°C. If a P_{H_2O} of 500 bars is assumed (*see* subsequent discussion of biotite composition), then an initial intrusion temperature of at least 850°C is probable.

An estimated temperature of 450°C, based on the composition of pyrrhotite, was cited previously. The occurrences of pyrrhotite at Rocky Hill suggest that it initially crystallized prior to the aplite stage and prior to pyrite. The estimated temperature may then merely reflect equilibrium, or apprpoach to equilibrium, with pyrite during the deuteric stage of falling temperatures, and may have no particular petrologic significance.

Oxygen Fugacity During Crystallization; The Significance of Biotite Composition and Mineral Assemblages

It is now commonly recognized that the course of crystallization and mineral paragenesis in igneous rocks is a function of oxygen fugacity in the magma as well as temperature and pressure of volatiles. A sufficient body of experimental work on synthetic systems and minerals, and upon some natural rocks, has been accumulated so that it is possible to estimate fairly accurately the conditions of oxygen fugacity under which crystallization occurred in many igneous rocks. An interpretation of changes in the mineral assemblages or in the composition of iron-bearing mineral phases within a plutonic body can often be made by comparison with the known effects of variation in oxygen fugacity during crystallization. Even more important, an accurate estimate of oxygen fugacity during the crystallization of a suitable mineral phase can make possible an estimation of other intensive parameters such as T and P_{H_2O} by comparison with appropriate phase-stability data.

A rough estimate of oxygen fugacity during crystallization of the Rocky Hill stock is provided by the co-existing mineral phase assemblage. Since magnetite is absent in only a relatively few rock samples, the prevailing indicator assemblage is quartz-magnetite-biotite-(sphene) for late stages in the paragenesis and quartz-magnetite-hornblende-(ilmenite-sphene) for somewhat earlier stages. Recent experimental work with oxygen buffers (Eugster and Wones, 1962; Wones and Eugster, 1965) indicates that the above mineral assemblages are compatible with oxygen fugacities in the range defined by the buffers quartz-fayalite-magnetite and magnetite-hematite. Late in the paragenesis of the granodiorite, the mineral assemblage of the sulfide-bearing rocks provides an independent indication of the range of oxygen fugacity. The assemblage pyrrhotite-magnetite-molybdenite-(biotite)-quartz-chalcopyrite can be compared with the data of Holland (1959, 1965); in the temperature interval 600° to 700°C the estimated range of oxygen fugacity is in good agreement with that defined by the buffers mentioned above. A more precise estimate of oxygen fugacity during the crystallization of biotite is obtained from experimental data which relates the partitioning of ferrous and ferric iron in biotite to oxygen fugacity (annite-"oxybiotite" proportions, Wones and Eugster, 1965, p. 1245, 1264). Relevant data for Rocky Hill biotites are summarized in Table 8. The compositions cited represent the averages of biotites co-existing with little or no magnetite (highest iron contents), and those co-existing with relatively large amounts of magnetite (lowest iron contents, *see* data in Table 3). These data indicate that the Rocky Hill biotites have "oxybiotite" contents consistent with oxygen fugacities slightly higher than those in equilibrium with the Ni-NiO buffer. Compared with biotites in equilibrium with oxygen fugacities of the Ni-NiO buffer, the Rocky Hill biotites will then be stable at slightly lower temperatures for any given $Fe/Mg+Fe$ ratio (all else being equal). The data of Table 8 also indicate that the biotites with lower total iron content crystallized in the presence of a relatively higher oxygen fugacity. Because of this relationship, it is likely that all of the Rocky Hill biotites crystallized at roughly the same temperatures.

In comparing the data of Table 8 with the biotite parameters experimentally determined by Wones and Eugster (1965), it must be remembered that the Rocky Hill biotites are not wholly members of the ternary system phlogopite-annite-"oxybiotite", but contain a siderophyllite or eastonite component (octahedral Al and Ti, *see* Table 1) as well as some anionic substitution of fluorine. The octahedral substitutions are not likely to decrease the stability of the Rocky Hill biotite relative to the phlogopite-annite series (Wones and Eugster, 1965, p. 1257), but the effect of fluorine substitution is unknown and has been neglected in this discussion. The potassium feldspar co-existing with biotite at Rocky Hill during magmatic crystallization may not have been a sanidine of the same thermal state as was present in the experimental work, and this factor has also not been considered. In spite of these limitations, the annite-"oxybiotite" ratios of biotites from Rocky Hill are considered to be a valid indication of oxygen fugacity. Estimates of T and P_{H_2O} from these

TABLE 8. AVERAGE COMPOSITIONS OF ROCKY HILL BIOTITE CO-EXISTING WITH LITTLE OR NO MAGNETITE AND CO-EXISTING WITH ABOUT 1 PERCENT MAGNETITE

	Weight %		mol fraction		$\dfrac{Fe^{**}}{Mg+Fe}$	$\dfrac{Fe^{3+}}{Fe^{2+}+Fe^{3+}}$
	FeO	Fe_2O_3	Annite*	Oxy-†Biotite		
Biotite with no magnetite	21.0	3.5	0.50	0.076	.576	0.13
Biotite with 1% magnetite	18.0	3.8	0.43	.082	.512	0.16

*Annite $= KFe_3^{+3}AlSi_3O_{10}(OH)_2$

†"Oxybiotite" $=KFe_3^{+3}AlSi_3O_{12}(H_{-1})$

**Mg + Fe equals total octahedral content

biotites, however, are subject to a greater degree of uncertainty because of these assumptions.

Figure 20 represents an estimate of the P_{H_2O} − T relationships for Rocky Hill biotite based upon an interpolation of the data of Wones and Eugster (1965) for oxygen fugacities of the hematite-magnetite and Ni-NiO buffers, and assumes co-existence with potassium feldspar and magnetite. The minimum melting curves for "granite" represent P_{H_2O} for a maximum and P = P_{H_2O} with 5 percent HF for a minimum (estimated) in temperatures at the liquidus minimum (Tuttle and Bowen, 1958; Wyllie and Tuttle, 1961). The inferred paragenesis at Rocky Hill indicates that biotite is late, and probably its crystallization persisted into the aplite stage. Thus the physical conditions during at least the last stages of biotite crystallization should be approximated by those of liquidus minima in the "granite" system. From Figure 20 biotite in the Rocky Hill granodiorite would appear to be stable at a P_{H_2O} in excess of 1 kb in the temperature range 690° to 725°C. Considering the assumptions involved, it is probable that the stability curve for Rocky Hill biotite in Figure 20 represents a maximum estimate for T (or minimum for P_{H_2O}).

The paragenesis at Rocky Hill may appear to introduce some qualifications in the use of Figure 20, for the crystallization of biotite, magnetite, and potassium feldspar did not proceed simultaneously (Fig. 9), nor was the potassium feldspar phase pure $KAlSi_3O_8$. Particularly in the core-facies granodiorite, potassium feldspar may co-exist with biotite only at a time when most of the latter phase has already crystallized. Because of several indications that biotite tends to remain in compositional equilibrium, or to recrystallize during its paragenesis, that is—(1) lack of zoning in microprobe analyses; virtually identical refractive index (γ) of grains from one rock sample, (2) evidence of growth of biotite in late fractures in essentially solid granodiorite, and (3) apparent equilibrium (or approach to it) with accessory phases which appear to be even later in paragensis, as in sample O-3E-2 (Table 3) which contains appreciable accessory sulfides—the paragenesis factor is not believed to introduce a significant bias in the estimated biotite stability data for Figure 20. However, the effect of purity of the potassium feldspar phase has not been evaluated. In view of the limitations previously mentioned upon the application of biotite composition data in estimating intensive physical parameters, further speculation upon the possible relationships of biotite composition to the crystallization sequence of the stock is obviously not warranted. Within these limitations, the estimated P-T stability data for bio-

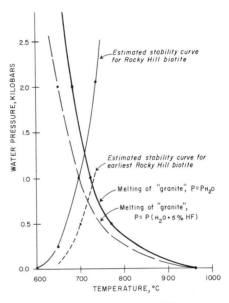

Figure 20. Estimated stability curves for Rocky Hill biotite and melting curves for "granite" with $P = P_{H_2O}$ and $P = P_{(H_2O + 5\% HF)}$.

tite at Rocky Hill (Fig. 20) are in good agreement with the T and P_{H_2O} estimates made in previous sections. The estimated stability data are considered to apply in the last stages of biotite crystallization, or at a point where reaction between biotite, magnetite, and potassium feldspar has become negligible.

In a previous paper (1965), the authors estimated initial water content of the magma on the basis of water content of the granodiorite, relative proportions of rim- and core-facies granodiorite, and matrix in the core-facies. The estimate of biotite stability, however, permits another means of speculating upon this property of the initial intrusion. The maximum temperature of crystallization for biotite of any composition would appear to be limited by the stability field of hornblende, but biotite near the compositions listed in Table 8 could exist at higher temperatures (or lower P_{H_2O}) prior to the crystallization of potassium feldspar (Wones and Eugster, 1965, p. 1249) due to the lower activity of $KAlSi_3O_8$ in the system. If, for example, the activity of $KAlSi_3O_8$ is less by 0.2, the biotite stability curve plotted in Figure 20 would be shifted to 700°C at 500 bars, as is shown by the dotted line. If the first biotite to crystallize was more phlogopitic, then the stability curve would be shifted to even higher temperatures. However, it does not appear reasonable to consider a P_{H_2O} less than 500 bars at the time of the initial appearance of biotite in the magma because of temperature limitations imposed by the (higher) initial temperature of the intrusion. Assuming that this P_{H_2O} is a minimum and that the magma is 40 percent crystals when biotite first appears, the initial water content of the magma would be in excess of approximately 1.3 weight percent at a minimum P_{H_2O} of 300 bars.[12]

EMPLACEMENT AND GENESIS OF MAGMA

In this section some of the various aspects of the field and petrographic data presented earlier will be discussed or interpreted from a geologic viewpoint. In general, the inferences or conclusions must be regarded as tentative; in some cases they are only an "educated guess." For ease of discussion and presentation, some new observational data (mainly geophysical) are also included here.

Form and Depth of the Stock—A Geophysical Interpretation

A gravity survey of the Rocky Hill vicinity was undertaken in an effort to obtain further information upon the depth and shape of the stock below the present ground surface. Stations were established at points of known elevation in the vicinity of the stock, and regional data for the area were furnished by the U.S. Geological Survey (H. W. Oliver, 1965, written commun.). The data were reduced to complete Bouguer values, using a density of 2.67 gms/cc and include corrections for terrain and curvature through Hayford Zone O (Swick, 1942, p. 67). A complete Bouguer gravity map of the Rocky Hill area is shown in Figure 21. The relative gravity "highs" are associated with outcrops of ultramafic rocks, metagabbro, and metavolcanic rocks. A general regional trend of decreasing gravity values eastward toward the Sierra Nevada and to the southwest in the San Joaquin Valley is apparent, and a strong deflection of the contours, which represents a gravity low, is present in the vicinity of the stock.

To provide a basis for estimating the distribution of the mass at depth, a gravity profile (Fig. 22) was constructed along the NNW-SSE cross-section line shown in Figure 21. A residual anomaly (Fig. 22) was obtained by removing the approximate regional trend from the observed anomaly. This profile indicates that there is a well-defined gravity low with a magnitude of more than 7 mgal approximately centered over the stock. Any error in estimation of the regional gravity gradient will have a relatively larger effect in the E-W dimension of Figure 21. Some uncertainty regarding the influence (minor) of surficial alluvium in Yokohl Valley on the east side of Rocky Hill also exists

[12]Weight percent—P_{H_2O} relationships are from Burnham and Jahns, 1962.

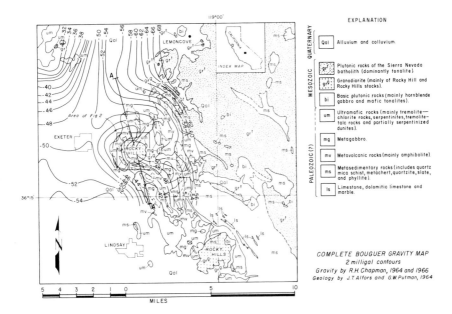

EXPLANATION

Qal	Alluvium and colluvium.
gr	Plutonic rocks of the Sierra Nevada batholith (dominantly tonalite).
grd	Granodiorite (mainly of Rocky Hill and Rocky Hills stocks).
bi	Basic plutonic rocks (mainly hornblende gabbro and mafic tonalites).
um	Ultramafic rocks (mainly tremolite—chlorite rocks, serpentinites, tremolite—talc rocks and partially serpentinized dunites).
mg	Metagabbro.
mv	Metavolcanic rocks (mainly amphibolite).
ms	Metasedimentary rocks (includes quartz mica schist, metachert, quartzite, slate, and phyllite).
ls	Limestone, dolomitic limestone and marble.

COMPLETE BOUGUER GRAVITY MAP
2 milligal contours
Gravity by R.H.Chapman, 1964 and 1966
Geology by J.T.Alfors and G.W.Putman, 1964

Figure 21. Complete Bouguer gravity map of the Rocky Hill area, Tulare County, California.

in Figure 21, and for these reasons the gravity profile was made along the line indicated.

Because the stock has a nearly-circular outline in plan, for a first approximation it was assumed that the anomalous mass has the shape of a vertical cylinder. A plot of the residual profile and the anomaly calculated for a vertical cylinder with a diameter of 7000 feet, a depth extent of 16,000 feet, and a density contrast of 0.19 gm/cc are shown in Figure 22. The density contrast of 0.19 gm/cc was arrived at by subtracting the density of the granodiorite (2.67 gm/cc) from a weighted average density of 2.86 gm/cc for the ultramafic and mafic country rocks. Except for the northwestern end of the anomaly the observed and theoretical profiles agree fairly well. The discrepancies at the northwest end of the anomaly may be caused by the uncertainty in removing the regional gravity trend in this part of the area. Thus, the gravity anomaly suggests that the intrusive mass is a diapir or piercement plug rather than a high-level projection of a larger and deeper plutonic mass.

It is doubtful that a more exact geophysical solution for the anomaly would have any real meaning because errors in the interpretation may result from several causes. These include the density contrast assumed, the relatively small number of gravity stations that define the anomaly, possible inaccuracies

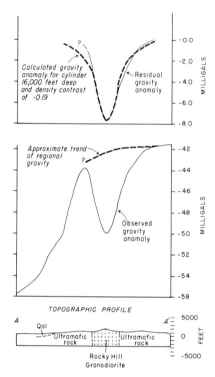

Figure 22. Gravity anomalies across the Rocky Hill stock.

in removing the regional gravity field, the presence of other nearby anomalies, and the large correction required for terrain in this area.

The depth extent indicated by the proposed model of the stock cannot be considered as an accurate estimate in view of the possible errors listed above. Also it is likely that the assumed density contrast will decrease with depth and thus require an even deeper and larger total mass to produce the observed residual anomaly. Although the shape of the proposed mass distribution is suggestive of a diapir or piercement plug, at least two possibilities exist to account for a loss of density contrast beneath any proposed mass model, and thus conceal the extent of the "root zone" of the stock.

One possibility is that below approximately 16,000 feet, the ultramafic-mafic wall rock assemblage is replaced by metasedimentary rocks similar to those exposed southeast of Rocky Hill. Another equally possible explanation is that the entire rock assemblage now exposed, including the stock, is truncated at that depth by the younger tonalite batholith exposed to the east. Granitic rocks are exposed in the Venice Hills seven miles northwest of Rocky Hill, and at other points to the north as well as in the main Sierra Nevada batholith to the east and southeast (Fig. 1). Thus, the existence of a regional, southwestward-dipping batholithic contact remains a possibility which is consistent with current geologic and geophysical data.

An estimate of the amount of the upper portion of the stock removed by erosion can only be a guess. The absence, however, of any deflection or shallowing of the plunge of lineation within the stock is suggestive of a level of exposure well below the roof of the pluton. We would accordingly estimate that at least 1 km has been removed from above the central part of the intrusion as it is now exposed. Combined with the gravity data on depth extent, a ratio of vertical axis length to horizontal diameter of at least 2.5 is suggested for the original pluton.

No other granitic rocks of a similar aspect are known to us in the area of Figure 1. The Rocky Hills (we regret the unfortunate similarity in locality names) pluton to the southeast near Lindsay (Fig. 1), although also a granodiorite, is petrographically, modally, and megascopically distinctly different. This fact, combined with the suggestion of the gravity data that the walls of the Rocky Hill stock do not diverge appreciably (but could converge) at depth, lead us to conclude that the stock is not a higher-level projection or derivative from some contemporaneous larger and deeper plutonic mass. This in no way affects the possibility that an extension of the younger tonalite batholith may, indeed, lie beneath the stock at a depth exceeding approximately 16,000 feet.

Mode of Emplacement

As mentioned earlier in the geologic description, structural evidence in the wall rocks bearing upon the mechanism of emplacement of magma appears to be lacking. Some parallelism of metagabbro and metavolcanic units imbedded in ultramafic rocks with the contacts of the stock occurs on the south and west margins (Fig. 2), but in general, planar structure is absent in most of the ultramafic rocks surrounding the stock. Although a widespread deflection of structural elements of the country rocks is thus not apparent, considerable evidence for magma movement during crystallization is evident in the protoclastic effects seen in the granodiorite. The approximately circular plan of the stock with steep walls indicates little or no directional resistance during magma emplacement, and the subvertical lineation present in the rock fabric indicates that at least the later stages of magma movement occurred along this direction. These observations appear to be most consistent with a vertical emplacement of magma by forceful intrusion. By forceful, we mean that the wall rocks were pushed outward and perhaps upward also, but no implication as to unusual magmatic or tectonic forces is intended. The ease with which serpentinized ultramafic rocks are deformed in conditions of tectonic stress is well recognized, regardless of the actual mechanism involved, and it appears quite likely that the ultramafic rocks yielded more or less uniformly in the horizontal plane during the intrusion of the Rocky Hill magma. The vertical rise of the magma as a diapir requires no other driving force than the observed density contrast, which would even be greater for granodiorite magma. The extent of rise of the intrusion, assuming the walls and roof are mainly ultramafic rocks, however, would be a function of loss of heat to the wall rocks and of viscosity of the magma. It is probable that some differential movement occurred within the magma, for a number of structural elements observed within the stock—that is, steeply dipping protoclastic shear zones and foliation, recrystallized mineral "slickenslides" on late fracture surfaces in rim-facies rocks, and persistence of steep mineral lineation in core-facies rocks—indicate that the interior portion continued to rise after the margins had become essentially solid.

Petrogenesis of the Magma and Relationship of the Rocky Hill Area to the Regional Geological Setting of the Sierra Nevada

A synthesis of recent data and an interpretation of the emplacement and structural evolution of the central part of the Sierra Nevada has been made by Bateman and others (1963). The southern boundary of this area lies some 30 miles to the north of Rocky Hill, but it would be amiss not to attempt some correlation of the geologic settings of the two areas, or to point out some apparent problems.

Although the isotopic ages of minerals from granitic rocks of the central Sierra Nevada almost uniformly range from 69 to 183 m.y., two distinct intrusive epochs, one in the general time interval 80 to 90 m.y. ago and another about 150 to 180 m.y. ago, have been postulated by Kistler and others (1965). In addition, a possible third intrusive epoch of intermediate age is represented by isolated plutons in the western Sierra Nevada with biotite ages of about 128 to 140 m.y.[13] (Curtis and others, 1958), and by pluton of the Klamath Mountains with biotite ages which range from 125 to 140 m.y. (Davis and others, 1965). The Rocky Hill stock appears to belong to the intermediate epoch on the basis of the biotite age of 132 (± 4) m.y. previously reported (Putman and Alfors, 1965). It is possible, however, that not all of these intermediate ages (which are based on K-Ar dating of biotite) are crystallization ages, and may prove to be too young when Rb-Sr or hornblende-based ages from these plutons are obtained.

An age of 109 (± 4) m.y. was obtained on biotite from a granodioritic facies of the main Sierra Nevada tonalite batholith 3.5 miles northeast of Rocky Hill (Putman and Alfors, 1965), and a potassium-argon age of 105.2 (± 3.6) m.y. was obtained on biotite from the Rocky Hills stock 6 miles southeast of Rocky Hill (Geochron Laboratories, Inc., 1967, written commun.). An age of 101 (± 5) m.y. was obtained on biotite from granodiorite of the "Dinkey Creek type," and an age of 105 (± 6) m.y. was obtained on hornblende from an amphibole schist within 600 feet of the contact with granodiorite of the "Dinkey Creek type;" both samples from T.11 S., R.25 E. in eastern Fresno County about 45 miles due north of Rocky Hill (R. A. Matthews and

---

[13]Original data recalculated with $\lambda_\epsilon = .585 \times 10^{-10}$ yr.$^{-1}$

J. T. Alfors, 1964, oral commun.). These ages are somewhat older than most of those found in the younger series of central Sierra Nevada plutons, but do compare well with ages determined on hornblende from granodiorite of the "Dinkey Creek type" reported by Bateman and others (1963) and Kistler and others (1965).

A clue to the sequence of events in the metamorphic rocks of the Rocky Hill area is provided by an indicated K-Ar age of 307 ($\pm$ 30) m.y. obtained from a tremolitic amphibole in metachert 1 mile north of Lindsay. The metachert is exposed as a large block (400 yards long) embedded in ultramafic rock and is 4 miles from the nearest outcrops of granitic rock. If this age is a reliable indication of Paleozoic metamorphism, it raises a number of problems in integrating the geology of the Sierra Nevada foothill belt in the vicinity of Rocky Hill with that of the western metamorphic belt flanking the central Sierra Nevada to the north. Although field evidence suggests that folding and metamorphism occurred during the Paleozoic, the most severe deformation involving tilting of Late Jurassic rocks and possible overthrusting of Paleozoic rocks in the western metamorphic belt occurred during the latest Jurassic (Bateman and others, 1963, p. D8). Serpentinites are frequently localized along steep fault zones, apparently in large part as a result of tectonic emplacement. It is possible that the belt of ultramafic rocks flanking Rocky Hill represents a southward extension of one of these zones, but if the ultramafic rocks were emplaced and metamorphosed during the Jurassic, then the Carboniferous K-Ar age of the included tectonic blocks, which should conform to the age of the latest metamorphism, is anomalous. Correlation with metamorphic rocks in the southern part of the western metamorphic belt mapped by Bateman and others (1963) is at present not possible because age designations there are uncertain, and the intervening area is one of granitic rocks. Obviously, more work is required, and we are at present unable to resolve the problem of relating metamorphic events in the Rocky Hill area to those further north in the Sierra Nevada foothill belt.

In comparison to the composition trends of plutonic rocks in the east-central Sierra Nevada (Bateman and others, 1963, p. D27-D33; Moore, 1963), which are generally calc-alkalic, the granodiorite of the Rocky Hill stock appears to be somewhat more silicic for the same ratio of K-feldspar/plagioclase, and to have a higher Na_2O/CaO ratio (that is the plagioclase is more sodic). In regard to the latter ratio, it is perhaps significant to note that plutonic rocks of the west-central Sierra Nevada, and the Klamath Mountains in particular, exhibit trondhjemitic differentiation tendencies, that is, soda enrichment (Davis and others, 1965), although this tendency may decrease somewhat southward in the plutonic rocks of the Sierra Nevada foothill belt (Fig. 23).

The silicic character of both the Rocky Hill granodiorite and the granodiorite of the Rocky Hills pluton to the south also contrasts with an apparent regional tendency for the silica and potassium contents of the Sierra Nevada granitic rocks to increase eastward (Moore, 1959; Moore and others, 1961). Visual examination of a number of stained-rock slabs from the tonalite batholith east of Rocky Hill (collected along a northwest-southeast distance of more

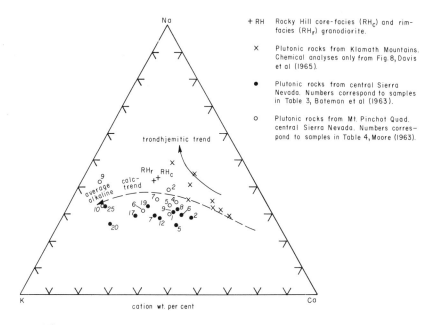

Figure 23. Ca-Na-K diagram for Rocky Hill core- and rim-facies granodiorite compared with plutonic rocks of the central Sierra Nevada and Klamath Mountains. The average calc-alkaline trend is from Nockolds and Allen (1953), and the trondhjemitic trend is from Larsen and Poldervaart (1961).

than 20 miles) reveals that it generally has a much lower content of quartz and potassium feldspar than the small granodiorite stocks to the west.

The data at hand are far from conclusive as to the source and evolution of magma which produced the Rocky Hill stock, but a few guesses can be made by extrapolating from the available data. We believe the majority of the inclusions in the Rocky Hill granodiorite are relicts of material that were not melted when the magma was formed. The diversity in texture and bulk composition of inclusions argues against an origin as autoliths of older border facies granodiorite, whereas the uniformity of mineralogy suggests that the inclusions have been in contact with the magma long enough to approach equilibrium with it. Trace element analyses presented earlier (Table 5) and the lack of a concentration of inclusions near the margins also strongly suggest that the inclusions were incorporated into the magma before intrusion to the present level. Finally, the similarity of the tiny opaque needle-like minerals in some plagioclase cores of both inclusions and granodiorite, and the similar appearance of these cores, suggests that both have a common parental affinity. A similar idea as to the origin of some or most of the inclusions in granitic plutons of the Mount Pinchot quadrangle (east-central Sierra Nevada) was suggested by Moore (1963, p. 118-121) on the basis of field relationships alone.

We envisage the Rocky Hill granodiorite magma as being generated by partial melting (anatexis) of predominantly metasedimentary rocks, with perhaps a minor contribution from basic metavolcanic rocks. The melting is regarded to be limited as much by the configuration of the parent rocks as by that of the isotherms in the crust. A localized source of magma generation for the Rocky Hill stock is indicated by the strong contrast in properties which exist between it and the nearest intrusive of similar rock type, the granodiorite stock at Rocky Hills near Lindsay (Fig. 1). This latter pluton is also silicic granodiorite, but in contrast to Rocky Hill granodiorites the rock is finer-grained and nonporphyritic, contains a more sodic plagioclase and accessory muscovite, and generally lacks hornblende. In spite of these differences, the Rocky Hills stock more closely resembles the Rocky Hill granodiorite than it does the large tonalite batholith to the east. Although the Rocky Hills pluton is apparently similar in age to the adjacent tonalite batholith and thus could be a differentiate from it, there is no field evidence to support this supposition, and differences in composition between these two intrusive bodies are more probably due to differences in the parent rocks from which the magmas were generated. The Rocky Hills stock lacks any observed aplites and contains an abundance of relatively mafic inclusions. Locally, the inclusions are so numerous as to constitute swarms embedded in a granodiorite matrix. The granodiorite is massive, and subvertical lineation is weak. These characteristics suggest to us that the Rocky Hill stock crystallized under a generally lower P_{H_2O} than prevailed at Rocky Hill, and that saturation of the magma in water probably did not occur during the course of crystallization.

Concluding Remarks

Quantitative regional data for many mineralogic and chemical variates have been used or sought in attempts to answer petrologic questions. In this paper, we have emphasized the regional aspects of trace metal content in a mineral phase as a means of providing information about the crystallization history of a small pluton. Some of the advantages of including trace element analyses in studies of regionally distributed chemical data in granitic rocks are as follows.

(1) Some granitic plutons are remarkably uniform in gross chemical and modal composition when random local variations are removed. There is usually more variation in the contents of trace elements, both locally and regionally, thus offering a possibility for distinguishing regional trends in fractionation or in the crystallization sequence of a pluton where the results of major element analyses or modal analyses are nonsignificant or ambiguous.

(2) Trace element assemblages of mineral phases in granitic rocks appear to be a characteristic and identifiable attribute of each individual plutonic unit (Putman and Burnham, 1963). Precise quantitative regional distribution data for such characteristic trace elements thus could be an aid in correlating genetically related units, or in separating composite units where field relations are uncertain, rock types are similar, and isotopic age determinations either lack sufficient precision or are influenced by subsequent thermal events.

The use of mineral phase trace element data is, however, not without complications. The most serious factor appears to be modally variable co-existing phases, such as the problem of co-existing magnetite which was treated here. For some purposes bulk rock trace element data is sufficient, and its use will avoid this problem. However, in some studies additional sample replication may be required to reduce the effects of local modal variation, and correspondingly more sensitive analytical procedures may be needed.

Our approach at Rocky Hill has often been empirical, with a somewhat limited study of local-scale variability. Replicate sampling was not made at all sample localities since the local-scale variability did not appear to constitute a problem in obtaining significant large-scale or regional ferromagnesian phase trace element data. As a consequence, this sample plan is inadequate for the determination of regional modal (except for magnetite) or bulk rock chemical data (this paper; Putman and Alfors, 1967). An empirical answer is thus provided for one of the questions posed by Whitten (1961) regarding the relevancy of a given sampling plan for the study of different variables, that is, a particular sampling plan adequate for the study of one or several variable attributes of a rock unit is not necessarily adequate for others, or even for the study of the same attributes in other rock units. The decision as to which of the variable properties of a rock body are to be studied may be dictated in advance by the definition or nature of a problem, but the sampling plan is governed by the nature of local variation. The spacing of sample localities then should be a function of the size or scale of the distribution features to be resolved. In practice, however, this requirement may be largely conditioned by such factors as degree of exposure, accessibility, and geologic setting of the rock body.

At Rocky Hill the essential features of the fractionation patterns for Ni, V, Cr, and Be could probably be obtained with half (possibly even fewer) the number of samples actually collected—but only at the risk of a possible loss of significance of the regional data for some elements because of increased variability at the within-grid scale. Collection of replicate samples at each grid locality would reduce the effects of this local variability, but cannot appreciably enhance the details of regional distributions of variables already shown to be significant. In this case, additional sample localities are needed to provide increased resolution, and at Rocky Hill this could possibly be helpful in interpreting the distributions of copper and modal magnetite and sulfides.

The Rocky Hill stock is *not* an unusual granitic body in terms of size, structure, or homogeneity of composition, nor is its geologic setting particularly unique. As such, it is unlikely that the characteristics of its chemical variability are grossly different from that of granitic rocks in general—at least in regard to source and mode of variation, if not in degree. Certainly the Rocky Hill stock does not represent any sort of extreme in the magnitude of variability of the properties analyzed, for it is a relatively homogeneous pluton with respect to many others—particularly those of composite batholiths and those with catazonal characteristics. Consequently, although this and other studies have provided significant regional variability data, it must be remembered that each plutonic unit may be unique in regard to the nature of scale-variability relationships.

At Rocky Hill we have attempted to provide a consistent pattern of petrologic relationships using various regional distributions developed from systematic sampling in a single pluton. Although our results can only be extrapolated to other plutons qualitatively, we hope this paper has provided the reader with some insight into the nature of some of the variability present in granitic rocks, and the effectiveness of quantitative regional distribution data in providing petrologic information. We do not wish to imply, however, any philosophy of determinism in granite petrology; that is, that significant regional distributions must necessarily be present in any plutonic body, or that an unambiguous interpretation of those present is always possible.

References Cited

Alfors, J. T., and Putman, G. W., 1965, Revised chemical analyses of traskite, verplanckite, and muirite from Fresno County, California: Am. Mineralogist, v. 50, p. 1500-1503.

—— 1966, Reconnaissance geologic map of parts of the Porterville, Lindsay, Exeter, Ivanhoe, Rocky Hill and Frazier Valley quadrangles, scale 1:24,000, and part of the Kaweah quadrangle, scale 1:62,500, *in* Matthews, R. A., and Burnett, J. L., *Compilers,* Fresno sheet, geologic map of California: California Div. Mines and Geology.

Alfors, J. T., Stinson, M. C., Matthews, R. A., and Pabst, A., 1965, Seven new barium minerals from eastern Fresno County, California: Am. Mineralogist, v. 50, p. 314-340.

Baird A. K., McIntyre, D. B., Welday, E. E., 1967a, Geochemical and structural studies in batholithic rocks of southern California: Pt. II, Sampling of the Rattlesnake Mountain Pluton for chemical composition, variability and trend analysis: Geol. Soc. America Bull., v. 78, p. 191-222.

Baird, A. K., McIntyre, D. B., Welday, E. E., and Baird, K. W., 1966, Regional chemical variations in batholithic rocks of southern California: Progress Report (Abstract): Geol. Soc. America Program, 1966 Annual Meetings, p. 8.

Baird, A. K., McIntyre, D. B., Welday, E. E., and Madlem, K. W., 1964, Chemical variations in a granitic pluton and its surrounding rocks: Science, v. 146, p. 258-259.

Baird, A. K., McIntyre, D. B., Welday, E. E., and Morton, D. M., 1967b, A test of chemical variability and field sampling methods, Lakeview Mountain Tonalite, Lakeview Mountains, Southern California Batholith, *in* Short Contributions to California Geology: California Div. Mines and Geology Spec. Rept. 92, p. 11-19.

Bateman, P. C., Clark, L. C., Huber, N. K., Moore, J. D., and Rinehart, C. D., 1963, The Sierra Nevada batholith—synthesis of recent work across the central part: U.S. Geol. Survey Prof. Paper 414D, 46 p.

Bateman, P. C., and Wahrhaftig, C., 1966, Geology of the Sierra Nevada, *in* Bailey, E. H., *Editor,* Geology of Northern California: California Div. Mines and Geology Bull. 190, p. 107-172.

Nockolds, S. R., and Allen, R., 1953, Geochemistry of some igneous rock series (Pt. 1): Geochim. et Cosmochim. Acta, v. 4, p. 105-142.

Noda, T., and Ushio, M., 1964, Hydrothermal synthesis of fluorine-hydroxyl-phlogopite: Pt. 2, Relationship between the fluorine content, lattice constants, and the conditions of synthesis of fluorine-hydroxyl-phlogopite: Geochemistry International, No. 1, p. 96-104.

O'Neil, R. L., and Suhr, N. H., 1960, Determination of trace elements in lignite ashes: Appl. Spectroscopy, v. 14, p. 45-50.

Peikert, E. W., 1962, Three-dimensional specific gravity variation in the Glen Alpine stock, Sierra Nevada, California: Geol. Soc. America Bull., v. 73, p. 1437-1442.

—— 1965, Model for three-dimensional mineralogical variation in granitic plutons based on the Glen Alpine stock, Sierra Nevada, California: Geol. Soc. America Bull., v. 76, p. 331-348.

Poldervaart, Arie, and Gilkey, A. K., 1954, On clouded plagioclase: Am. Mineralogist, v. 39, p. 75-91.

Putman, G. W., and Alfors, J. T., 1965, Depth of intrusion and age of the Rocky Hill stock, Tulare County, California: Geol. Soc. America Bull., v. 76, p. 357-364.

—— 1967, Frequency distribution of minor metals in the Rocky Hill stock, Tulare County, California: Geochim. et Cosmochim. Acta, v. 31, p. 431-450.

Putman, G. W., and Burnham, C. W., 1963, Trace elements in igneous rocks, northwestern and central Arizona: Geochim. et Cosmochim. Acta, v. 27, p. 53-106.

Rankama, K., and Sahama, Th. G., 1950, Geochemistry: Chicago, Chicago Univ. Press, 912 p.

Richmond, J. F., 1965, Chemical variation in quartz monzonite from Cactus Flat, San Bernardino Mountains, California: Am. Jour. Sci., v. 263, p. 53-63.

Rogers, A. F., 1937, Introduction to the study of minerals, 3rd edition: New York, McGraw-Hill Book Co., 626 p.

Slemmons, D. B., 1962, Determination of volcanic and plutonic plagioclase using a three- or four-axis universal stage: Geol. Soc. America Spec. Paper 69, 64 p.

Smith, J. V., and Gay, P., 1958, The powder patterns and lattice parameters of plagioclase feldspars II: Mineralogical Mag., v. 31, p. 744-762.

Stewart, D. B., 1958, System $CaAl_2Si_2O_8$-SiO_2-H_2O (Abstract): Geol. Soc. America Bull., v. 69, p. 1648.

Swick, C. H., 1942, Pendulum gravity measurements and isostatic reductions: U. S. Coast and Geod. Survey Spec. Pub. 232, 82 p.

Taubeneck, W. H., 1957, Geology of the Elkhorn Mountains, northeastern Oregon: Bald Mountain batholith: Geol. Soc. America Bull., v. 68, p. 181-238.

Taubeneck, W. H., 1964, Cornucopia stock, Wallowa Mountains, northeastern Oregon-Field relations: Geol. Soc. America Bull., v. 75, p. 1093-1115.

Toulmin, Priestly, III, and Barton, P. B., Jr., 1964, A thermodynamic study of pyrite and pyrrhotite: Geochim. et Cosmochim. Acta, v. 28, p. 641-671.

Turner F. J., and Verhoogen, J., 1960, Igneous and metamorphic petrology, 2nd edition: New York, McGraw-Hill Book Co., 694 p.

Tuttle, O. F., 1949, Two pressure vessels for silicate-water studies: Geol. Soc. America Bull., v. 60, p. 1727-1729.

Tuttle, O. F., and Bowen, N. L., 1958, Origin of granite in the light of experimental studies in the system $NaAlSi_3O_8$-$KAlSi_3O_8$-SiO_2-H_2O: Geol. Soc. America Mem. 74, 154 p.

Tuttle, O. F., and Jahns, R. H. (in prep., 1968), Genesis of homogeneous aplite dikes.

Vance, J. A., 1957, Coalescent growth of plagioclase grains in igneous rocks (Abstract): Geol. Soc. America Bull., v. 68, p. 1849.

―――― 1961, Polysynthetic twinning in plagioclase: Am. Mineralogist, v. 46, p. 1097-1119.

Welday E. E., and Baird, A. K., 1966, Use of grain-mount thin sections in modal mapping (Abstract): Geol. Soc. America Program 1966 Annual Meetings, p. 239.

Welday, E. E., Baird, A. K., McIntyre, D. B., and Madlem, K. W., 1964, Silicate sample preparation for light-element analyses by X-ray spectrography: Am. Mineralogist, v. 49, p. 889-903.

Whitten, E. H. T., 1959, Composition trends in a granite: modal variation and ghost-stratigraphy in part of the Donegal granite, Eire: Jour. Geophys. Research, v. 64, p. 835-848.

―――― 1961, Quantitative areal modal analysis of granitic complexes: Geol. Soc. America Bull., v. 72, p. 1331-1360.

Whitten, E. H. T., and Boyer, R. E., 1964, Process-response models based on heavy-mineral content of San Isabel Granite, Colorado: Geol. Soc. America Bull., v. 75, p. 841-862.

Wones, D. R., and Eugster, H. P., 1965, Stability of biotite: experiment, theory and application: Am. Mineralogist, v. 50, p. 1228-1272.

Wyllie, P. J., and Tuttle, O F., 1961, Experimental investigation of silicate systems containing two volatile components—Pt. 2, The effects of NH_3 and HF, in addition to H_2O on the melting temperatures of aplite and granite: Am. Jour. Sci., v. 259, p. 128-143.

Yoder, H. S., Jr., Stewart, D. B., and Smith, J. R., 1957, Ternary feldspars: Annual Report of Director of Geophysical Laboratory, 1956-57, Carnegie Institution of Washington, p. 206-214.

Youden, W. J., 1951, Statistical methods for chemists: New York, John Wiley & Sons, 126 p.

Appendix I

DETAILS OF ANALYTICAL METHODS USED IN THIS STUDY

Spectrochemical Analyses

Trace element analysis procedure for ferromagnesian mineral separates was similar to that described by O'Neil and Suhr (1960), using lutetium as an internal standard for Ba, Be, Cr, Fe, Mg, Ni, V, and Y, and germanium for Ag, Cu, Sn and Zn. Magnetite and sphene separates were buffered with a mixture of SiO_2, Al_2O_3, MgO and K_2SO_4 or SiO_2 and K_2SO_4, respectively, to promote arcing conditions similar to those of the ferromagnesian phases. Standards include a series of prepared synthetic powders approximating biotite in composition, and natural rock standards U.S.G.S. W-1 and G-1, CAAS syenite and sulfide, and Msusule Tonalite T-1. Agreement between these standards in constructing calibration curves was highly satisfactory, and indicated that little differential matrix effect was to be expected in the composition ranges of materials analyzed.

All $\frac{1}{8}$ inch electrodes were arced in a Stallwood jet with a linear ceramic orifice. This orifice requires no enclosing dome or jacket to remove air from the arc gap and constrains the arc to a narrow column, which helps to improve precision. Estimates of the precision of this method are included in the text, Table 4.

Major constituent analyses of rocks and minerals followed the method of Joensuu and Suhr (1962), with the substitution of $Li_2B_4O_7$ as the fusion medium to enable the analysis of sodium. This analytical method has provided good precision in other studies (Alfors and others, 1965) and commonly yields a coefficient of variation in the range 2 to 5 percent for a single determination.

Fluorine analyses of selected biotite concentrates utilized the SrF band at 5772 Å. Electrodes were loaded with a 1:1:2 mixture of biotite, $SrCO_3$, and graphite, and arced in a conventional jet with argon-oxygen. Thallium (5350.5 Å) precipitated from solution onto graphite was used as an internal standard. For analyses of fluorine in biotite the SrF band is more sensitive than the CaF band at 5291 Å which is more commonly used. Small amounts of calcium (that is, <2 percent CaO) from minor hornblende included with the biotite, or as a constituent of the biotite do not appear to have any effect upon the intensity of the

99

SrF band. Results of replicate determinations indicate that the coefficient of variation is 7 to 8 percent.

A summary of operating conditions for the spectrochemical analyses is given in Appendix Table 1.

X-ray Spectrographic Analyses

All X-ray spectrographic analyses were performed with a Norelco vacuum spectrometer and tungsten tube. Analysis of iron and potassium in bulk rock samples followed the procedure of Welday and others (1964), except that in lieu of pelletizing, the borate fusions were poured as discs and analyzed directly. Potassium and rubidium analyses of ferromagnesian separates and feldspars were made directly on mineral powders. Standards were prepared from the natural rock samples referred to under the previous section, as well as synthetic mixes fused in lithium tetraborate. Precision of the bulk rock analyses is generally better

APPENDIX TABLE I. SPECTROGRAPHIC OPERATING CONDITIONS

Excitation	Mineral Separate Trace Element, Fe, Mg Analyses	Major Constituent Analyses	Fluorine Analyses
Electrodes Sample	Ultra Carbon Type 5790	Ultra Carbon Type 5185	Ultra Carbon Type 3417
Counter	Ultra Carbon Type 5001	Ultra Carbon 5001	National L3957
Current, Amp.	11	11	10
Gas	Argon/Oxygen 80:20	CO_2	Argon/Oxygen 80:20
Flow rate	6 1./min.	5 1./min.	6.5 1./min.
Exposure	To Completion	To Completion	30 Sec.
Emulsion	Kodak SA-1	Kodak SA-1	Kodak III-F
Spectrograph	Jarrell-Ash 3.4 meter, Ebert Mount, 15000 lines/in grating		
Wave length Range	3000-4275 Second order	2200-3500 First Order	4900-6200 First Order
Slit Width (μ)	16	12	16
Filter	Corning Glass with 2900 Å cut off (removes 3rd order interference)	#30 mesh screen for intensity reduction	Plate Glass with 3100 Å cut off
Intensity Control and Calibration	4-Step Sector, Log Step Factor of 0.4, Calibration by Two Step Method using internal standard and analysis lines.		

than a coefficient of variation of 2 percent. The indicated precision for the Rb/K ratios in mineral separates is a coefficient of variation of 5 percent or less.

Ferrous-Ferric Iron Analyses

Analyses of ferric and ferrous iron were made on selected bulk rock samples and ferromagnesian mineral separates. Samples were digested in HF and H_2SO_4, and were titrated for ferrous iron with $K_2Cr_2O_7$ using sodium diphenylamine as an indicator in a solution buffered with boric and phosphoric acids. Reduction was made in a Jones silver reductor, and total iron as Fe^{2+} was titrated similarly. Ferric iron was determined by difference. Replicate determinations indicate a precisions within .05 percent FeO.

Ignition Loss and Water Determinations

Ignition loss runs were made on several bulk rock samples and biotite separates in order to estimate water content. Sample charges of 30 to 75 mg were loaded in gold capsules crimped to leave a pinhole and placed in covered graphite holders buffered with iron to prevent oxidation (Alfors and Putman, 1965). All runs were made at approximately 980°C in an electric furnace. Simultaneous runs on charges of pure quartz served as a blank. Provided that the contents of carbonates and sulfides in the sample are low, this method appears to yield satisfactory estimates of water content in most granitic rocks or their constituent minerals.

Specific Gravity Measurements

The specific gravity of bulk rock samples was determined on a direct-reading-beam balance of the type designed by Rogers (1937, p. 137-138) with a distance of 68 cm between the fulcrum and counterpoise. Samples ranged from 300 to 500 grams in weight. Using water as the immersion medium, the sensitivity of the balance is 0.002 gm/cc, and the precision on duplicate runs was better than ±0.005 in the density range 2.6 to 2.7.

Magnetic Susceptibility Determinations

Measurements of the magnetic susceptibility of crushed rock samples were used to determine the magnetite content of all granodiorite samples. Splits of each jaw-crushed rock sample were loaded in 32 mm diameter glass vials and inserted in the coil well of a magnetic susceptibility bridge. The balance point was determined visually with an oscilloscope, and the resistance differential (ΔR) was used directly to estimate magnetite content. Calibration was provided by means of splits of 16 pulverized samples from which the magnetite was removed magnetically and weighed. This method has a sensitivity of about 0.02 weight percent magnetite, and duplicate sample splits were reproducible within a range of less than ±5 percent of the average amount present, a precision which was quite adequate in relation to the total range of magnetite contents encountered.

Gravity Measurements

Gravity measurements in the Rocky Hill area were made with a Worden Gravity meter have a sensitivity of 0.01 milligal per vernier scale division. Field readings were reproducible within a range of .03 to .04 milligal. Terrain corrections (of individual readings) were carried out to a 100-mile radius, that is, Hayford Zone O (Swick, 1942).

Appendix II

CORRECTION OF FERROMAGNESIAN TRACE ELEMENT ANALYSES FOR CO-EXISTING MAGNETITE

Because of bias induced by the presence of variable amounts of magnetite, raw analytical data for the ferromagnesian phases cannot be used directly to study regional composition trends. In this work, the reference state for data comparison was arbitrarily chosen as one where magnetite is absent, that is, a zero magnetite content. A correction for the amount of co-existing magnetite was therefore applied to the ferromagnesian phase trace element data from all sample localities prior to the derivation of the trend surfaces of Figures 12 to 14, 16, and 17. A procedure for accomplishing this correction is illustrated below:

Average Content $(\overline{X})$ of Ferromagnesian Samples with:

A. About 1 weight percent magnetite		B. Little or no magnetite
Cr	28.2	39.1
Cu	115	64.6
Ni	60.4	48.7
V	378	478.4
Zn	458.3	410.9
Number of Samples	(18)	(16)

Thus, in the case of vanadium, for example, an average difference (ΔX) of approximately 100 ppm V in the ferromagnesian phase results from the presence of 1 weight percent magnetite in the sample. A correction on the basis of 10 ppm V per each 0.1 weight percent magnetite was therefore *added* to the analyzed V content of each ferromagnesian separate in deriving data to be compared on the basis of a zero magnetite content. This addition is necessary since magnetite has a much higher V content than the ferromagnesian phases (*see* Table 5), and thus, if absent, leaves more V to be incorporate by these phases. Similar additions or subtractions were made for other elements depending upon whether the magnetite has a higher (V, Cr) or lower (Ni, Cu, Zn) content relative to the ferromagnesian phase.

A check upon the validity of this approach is provided by the proportions and compositions of the phases themselves. If the iron in 1 weight percent of magnetite is used to form biotite (with a composition such as that found in samples with little or no magnetite; Table 2), then about 3.5 weight percent additional biotite would result. Again using vanadium as an example for illustration of the calculation, the following balance can be shown, assuming a rock composition of constant total iron.

I. Rock with About 1 Weight Percent Magnetite

The average ferromagnesian phase content of granodiorite samples with 1 weight percent magnetite is approximately 7 weight percent. Using this figure, the vanadium content of the rock is then:

7 percent biotite x 378 ppm V	= 26.4
1 percent magnetite x 2350 ppm V[14]	= 23.5
	49.9 ppm.

II. Rock with Little or No Magnetite

10.5 percent biotite x 478.4 ppm V	= 50.3 ppm.

Similar calculations were made to check the adjustments made for other elements, and in some cases the corrections were refined slightly by comparing mean ferromagnesian trace element analyses for magnetite contents other than 1 percent. Although minor hornblende is present in many ferromagnesian mineral separates, no separate adjustment was made since the original trace element analytical data was obtained from such phase mixtures. Although the magnetite at Rocky Hill has little or no beryllium, no correction was applied to the ferromagnesian phase data for Figure 15 since the co-existing feldspars of the granodiorite constitute a larger "reservoir" for this element. In this regard, possibly the fact that the area of low beryllium contents in Figure 15 does not coincide exactly with those of Figures 12 to 14, is a reflection of bias introduced by the presence of variable amounts of hornblende in the ferromagnesian separates (hornblende has a higher Be content than the co-existing biotite—Table 5). However, if such an effect exists, no adjustment could be made since separate hornblende analyses were not made, and since the determination of modal hornblende lacks adequate precision (Table 3).

As a sequel to earlier work on the frequency distribution of the trace metals in the Rocky Hill stock (Putman and Alfors, 1967), it should be noted that the magnetite compensated data for Cr, Ni, V, and Zn show an even closer approach to lognormal distributions than the original raw data.

---

[14]Mean V content of analyzed magnetite from samples with approximately 1 weight percent.

Appendix III

HYDROTHERMAL EXPERIMENT METHODS AND RESULTS

The experiments were carried out in externally heated cold-seal pressure vessels (Tuttle, 1949; Luth and Tuttle, 1963). The temperatures are believed to be accurate within $\pm 10°C$ and pressures are believed to be accurate to ± 0.2 kb. Runs were quenched by removing the external furnace and directing a jet of air against the pressure vessel.

Starting materials for the runs were powdered aplite (10S-1E) and granodiorite (2N-7W) and their fused equivalents (Appendix Table 2, runs 3 and 4). Chemical analyses of the aplite and granodiorite are given in a previous paper (Putman and Alfors, 1965, Table 1).

All runs were made by sealing a known amount of glass or crystals and water into gold or platinum tubes. The total charge weighed about 10 mg, 25 $\pm$ 5 percent of which was water. The products of each run were examined with a microscope and by X-ray powder diffraction. Results are given in Appendix Table 2 (*see* following page).

APPENDIX TABLE 2.   RESULTS OF HYDROTHERMAL RUNS ON ROCKY HILL APLITE*
AND GRANODIORITE†

Run	Starting material	P,kb	T,°C	Time, hours	Results**
25	FA	1	700	46	Q+P+K?+G+V
27	PA	1	700	46	Q+P+K+V?+B
21	FA	1	750	51	P+G+V
23	PA	1	750	51	Q+P+G+V+B
13	FA	1	800	26	G+V+B?
15††	PA	1	800	26	Q+G+B
5	FA	1	850	24	G+V
7	PA	1	850	24	G+V
2	PA	1	900	2	Q+G+V+O
3	PA	1	1185	15	G+V
29	FA	2	700	56	G+V
31	PA	2	700	56	Q+P+G+V+O
17	FA	4	650	66	Q+G+V+B
19*	PA	4	650	66	Q+P+K+B
9	FA	4	700	40	G+V+B+H?+O
11	PA	4	700	40	G+V+B+O
26	FGd	1	700	46	Q+P+K+G?+V+H+O
28	PGd	1	700	46	Q+P+B+H
22	FGd	1	750	51	Q+P+G+V+H+O
24	PGd	1	750	51	Q+P+K+V+B+H+O
14	FGd	1	800	26	P+G+V?+H?
16	PGd	1	800	26	P+G+V+H+O
6	FGd	1	850	24	G+V+B?+H?+O
8	PGd	1	850	24	G+V+H+O
1	PGd	1	900	2	P+G+V+H
4	PGd	1	1185	15	G+V
30	FGd	2	700	56	Q+P+G+V+H?
32	PGd	2	700	56	Q+P+K+G+V+B+H
18	FGd	4	650	66	Q+P+K+G?+O
20	PGd	4	650	66	Q+P+B+H
10	FGd	4	700	40	Q+P+G+H
12	PGd	4	700	40	Q+P+B+H

*Aplite from near 10S-1E
†Granodiorite from near 2N-7W
**Identified phases; small amounts of glass and potassium feldspar in particular are diffi-
cult to detect.
††May not have been saturated with water

P = plagioclase, K = potassium feldspar, Q = quartz, G = glass, V = vapor, H_2O-rich
fluid phase, B = biotite, H = hornblende, O = opaques, FA = fused aplite, PA = powdered aplite, FGd = fused granodiorite, PGd = powdered granodiorite

Index